How to Be a

Permanent

TEMP

Winning
Strategies for
Surviving in
Today's
Workplace

By
Joan Damico

CAREER
PRESS
Franklin Lakes, NJ

How to Be a Permanent Temp
Edited by Kristen Mohn
Typeset by Eileen Dow Munson
Cover design by Rob Johnson
Printed in the U.S.A. by Book-mart Press

To order this title, please call toll-free 1-800-CAREER-1 (NJ and Canada: 201-848-0310) to order using VISA or MasterCard, or for further information on books from Career Press.

The Career Press, Inc., 3 Tice Road, PO Box 687, Franklin Lakes, NJ 07417
www.careerpress.com

Library of Congress Cataloging-in-Publication Data

Damico, Joan, 1962-
    How to be a permanent temp : winning strategies for surviving in today's
workplace / by Joan Damico.
        p. cm.
    Includes bibliographical references and index.
    ISBN 1-56414-561-1 (paper)
        1. Temporary employment—United States. 2. Temporary employees. I. Title.

    HD5854.2.U6 D35 2001
    650.14—dc21

                                                                                    2001035362

*To Bob Bly,
my mentor and inspiration
both in person and
through your many helpful books.*

Acknowledgments

My special thanks to Howard Ross for sacrificing many nights and weekends to help give the book its unique perspective. Howard's more than 23 years' experience in team building, organizational consulting, staffing, and training have been a tremendous boost in uncovering a wider range of permanent temping opportunities. Combining his extensive human resources background with a visionary outlook and entrepreneurial sprit has earned Howard executive level positions with major national interim executive placement and outsourcing staff augmentation firms. His knowledge and experience not only validate this new state of employment, but also have helped shape it into a lucrative, satisfying business for many interim and contingent employees. Howard, you're a delight to work with.

My gratitude to the permanent temps who've taken time to share their experiences with me, especially Chris Moore, Janet Ruhl, "Dinosaur," and Ken Norkin; I'm gratified by your honesty and candor that not only helped me write the book, but also will help would-be permanent temps. All the best to you.

Every writer has at least one coach and inspiration. Thanks to Rich Persen for awakening the writer in me.

And of course, to my husband, Marc, thank you for your love and encouragement without which this book would not have been possible.

Contents

Preface

Today's workforce has undergone dramatic changes. Temping, once thought of as something to fill the gap between full-time jobs or a clerical level function, can now be found in nearly all industries and professional disciplines. It's the new way of working in a dynamic business environment.

In an interview with Ework Exchange, Dr. Robert B. Reich, former U.S. Secretary of Labor, described the changing employee affiliation in the "new economy" as being project-based as opposed to organization-based. He suggests that people will move from one project to the next on the same or different team and individual earnings will be based on skills and the demand for those skills instead of your position within an organization. With a greater emphasis on skills and project related assignments, temporary employment provides a more efficient capacity utilization of human capital.

The widespread use of PCs and the Internet has created a glut in a variety of knowledge-based positions. A recent surge in merger and acquisition activity and IPOs has created the need for temporary executive level expertise. The demand for skilled workers continues in nearly all functional areas throughout organizations.

The U.S. Bureau of Labor Statistics shows satisfaction among 84 percent of the over eight million independent contractors in 1999. In another poll conducted by the Freelance Work Exchange Web site for the week of October 2, 2000, 73 percent of respondents preferred $50,000 in freelance contracts to an $80,000 per year full-time job. Never before have there been so many unique employment opportunities. Yet, how do we harness these opportunities?

Based on the U.S. Department of Labor Bureau of Labor Statistics's 1997 study "Are Workers More Secure?" over 48 percent of contingent workers voluntarily chose their work arrangement due to personal reasons such as family obligations, flexible work schedule, and enrollment in school. While the motives for becoming a temp are as varied as the temping profession itself, often prospective temps lack a proactive strategy and their experience is hampered either by financial strife or an overall bad experience.

How to Be a Permanent Temp provides an easy-to-follow strategy for minimizing risk, maximizing earnings, enhancing job satisfaction, and adding to your professional experience portfolio. It's a guide to earning a living while obtaining job satisfaction and diversity as a permanent temporary professional. It provides useful information on how to seek temporary employment, how the hiring process works in a temporary environment, and common pitfalls to avoid.

Welcome to the future of agile organizations and contingent staffing and employment opportunities.

Introduction

Most people think of a job or the idea of "work" in the traditional sense—a fixed period of time, usually 9 a.m. until 5 p.m., spent in an office under the direct employ of a company whose name and logo appear each week on a paycheck. While that may be the case for the majority of the workforce, a growing number are redefining a job, or "work," as a collection of specific skills and attributes that one markets directly or indirectly to companies on a project or contingent basis.

How do the two definitions differ? The former focuses on job titles in relation to specific organizational hierarchies. For example, you're a materials' process engineer for XYZ Corporation, and the job description defines your responsibilities, reporting structure, skills required, etc. as they relate to the XYZ Corporation's organizational structure. Your compensation is based on industry standards and corporate policies and is usually paid on a weekly or bimonthly basis.

In the latter definition, you define yourself by the skills you possess and how they relate to a specific project, independent of organizational hierarchy. Compensation is based on an hourly rate or project fee and is usually paid on project start and/or at intervals throughout the project. If you are affiliated with a temporary employment agency, then your compensation may be paid weekly or bimonthly for the duration of the assignment. Using the above example in the context of a temporary assignment, the materials process engineer embarks on an assignment for a company seeking to implement a new production facility. The assignment would be temporary, but long-term in the sense that the engineer will work eight to 12 months on-site to facilitate the implementation for a fixed fee or hourly rate.

You're probably wondering why the company would hire an outside consultant to perform this important function. Therein lies a key advantage of temping from the employer's perspective— if a company doesn't have the in-house skills, manpower, or can't accomplish the task cost effectively, then outsourcing offers an appealing alternative. Temps offer a cost-effective means to quickly complete various projects without adding to corporate overhead or training expenses.

But from the temp's perspective, the benefits are even more appealing. Not only do you use the job skills and professional attributes you enjoy most, but you also choose the assignments on which you want to work. And in many cases, the compensation is greater than what you would be earning as a full-time employee. Temping lets you focus on what you do best without all the distractions associated with a full-time job such as corporate politics, fitting in, putting in "face time," jumping through hoops to hopefully climb the next step on corporate ladder, and putting your personal life aside for the good of the company.

Temping puts *you* in control of your career. You are less dependent on an employer for your career growth and financial well-being. For many, the ideal of "job security" doesn't exist in today's corporate culture that is always in the state of flux—reorganizing, downsizing, right sizing, reengineering, restructuring, or whatever the latest buzzword is.

Permanent temps have discovered that sacrificing the regular weekly paycheck affords them more opportunities to grow and learn by working for a variety of companies on a contingent basis.

More importantly, permanent temps take on as little or as much as they desire to achieve a more fulfilling work/life balance than is possible under the rigid guidelines of the corporate world.

How to Be a Permanent Temp guides you through the process of becoming a permanent temp so that you can capitalize on temping opportunities.

Still curious? Take the quiz in Chapter 1 to see if temping is right for you.

1
So, You're Interested in Joining the Contingent Workforce...

Are you ready to take control of your career? Do you seek new and different work experience? Perhaps you're testing a new career. *How to Be a Permanent Temp* is your guide to success in the workforce of tomorrow. In this book, you'll explore your options, determine your goals, and develop an action plan that will not only help you achieve your goals, but also ensure your success in the temporary workforce.

Temping is no longer used to fill a gap between full-time positions. Temping is the new way to work and capitalize on the skills that you possess. While temping is not for everyone, its flexibility and empowerment are a powerful draw for many who prefer to control their own destiny.

How Will I Know If Temping Is Right For Me?

Let's discover if you have what it takes to thrive in the temporary work culture. Take the short quiz below to determine if you're a good candidate for the permanent temp lifestyle.

1. Do you have a specific technical skill or business acumen? (For example, do you know programming languages; are you experienced in relocating manufacturing facilities or in mergers and acquisitions?)

2. Are you entrepreneurial? (For example, do you enjoy taking charge, analyzing information, uncovering new opportunities, and making daily business decisions?)

3. Do you work well independently; are you self-motivated and vision oriented?

4. Do you have the personal strength to take control of your career? (Are you empowered by independence?)

5. Are you risk/reward motivated? (Keep in mind that rewards may not necessarily be monetary. The reward could be a flexible workday.)

6. Are you comfortable without a fixed weekly paycheck?

7. Do you easily meld into a variety of corporate cultures? (For example, could you work equally as well in the thrill and sometimes chaotic nature of a startup and in a more structured, well-established organization?)

8. Are you willing to travel and/or relocate? (What's the geographical area in which you're willing to travel to promote yourself? For example, if you're a hot-shot Web developer, are you willing to travel to the high-tech regions such as Silicon Valley for opportunities?)

9. Are you technology savvy? (Can you use a computer for documents, spreadsheets, presentations, sending and retrieving e-mail, and locating information on the Internet?)

10. Do you have good presentation skills with which to promote yourself?

11. Do you have personal organization skills and the ability to run your own business?

12. Can you network?

Probability of success as a permanent temp:

Number of "yes" responses	Probability
10-12	Very high
6-9	Medium to high
0-5	Low

Save your answers, we'll consult them again later when we explore the types of temping arrangements available.

If you completed the questionnaire and it indicates that you've got what it takes, then read on. If you're not considered an ideal candidate, read on to learn more about what it takes to thrive in the world of temporary employment.

First, let's take a look at various job functions and determine which one best describes your experience and skills. Don't become preoccupied with titles as they can span several functional roles and the titles are often defined within the context of the size and scope of an organization. The chart on page 18 lists key job functions and a sampling of job titles that fit within each.

Temporary, Freelance, Consultant, and Contract— What's the Difference?

These terms are frequently used interchangeably. Generally, recruiters use the following guidelines to describe typical work arrangements:

❖ Temp: administrative, clerical, or light industrial professionals.

❖ Interim: executive professionals.

❖ Freelance: creative professionals.

❖ Consultant and Independent Contractor: technical/ managerial/professionals.

The term "permanent temp" is used to encompass all of these work arrangements regardless of title. It's important to note that according to U.S. government classifications, all of the above fall under one of two categories:

1. W2: an "employee" who is potentially eligible for benefits and is paid directly by the company or a third party (albeit an agency) and is having federal income taxes withheld by the employer or third party.

FUNCTION		
Executive/managerial	Knowledge-based specialists (professional/technical/managerial)	Implementers (administrative, technicians, professionals, paraprofessionals)
DESCRIPTION		
People with a strategic vision that utilize information to make *mission critical* decisions. Simply put, their overall business savvy tells them that there are issues, but they don't know exactly where or what they are. Once informed, they're able to make the decision on how to resolve the issues.	People with an expertise in a particular field or specialty who gather and analyze information, then make recommendations based on their analysis. Simply put, they uncover the issues and make recommendations on how best to handle them. They don't decide on the best resolution nor do they resolve the issues.	Specialists who are responsible for completing specific tasks that support a given cause. In other words, they possess the skills to complete the tasks that resolve the issues uncovered by the knowledge-based specialists upon strategic decisions made by the executive/managerial function.
TITLES		
CEOs, CIOs, CFOs, business development, presidents and executive vice presidents of functional areas such as marketing and sales or strategic business units and geographic regions.	Human resource analysts, market analysts, financial analysts, systems analysts, chief marketing officer, help desk technicians, diagnostician, *doctors, *lawyers (roles that deal with the analytics of information).	Project managers, plant managers, technicians, software programmers, accountants, middle managers, clerical and administrative professionals.

*These professions can also be found under the implementer category, as certain specialists not only verify a diagnosis, but also possess the skills to resolve the issues. For example, a general practitioner may suspect a herniated disk. The patient would be referred to an orthopedic specialist who would verify the diagnosis, suggest the remedy, and conduct the surgery to correct the problem.

Figure 1.1

2. 1099: an independent contractor or sole proprietor who is not eligible for employee benefits and invoices the company directly for services rendered and pays taxes directly to the IRS via quarterly estimated payments.

The government classifies you based on the "substance of the relationship" with the employer, not the label. W2 and 1099 refer to the tax form you'll receive from your employer/client at the end of the year. According to the IRS, a W2 status can represent a full-time employee of a given company or an independent contractor working for a professional services agency. A 1099 status represents an independent contractor when the employer controls or directs only the result of the work and not the means and methods for accomplishing the result. So, according to the IRS *Publication 15A*, even though you're labeled an independent contractor, you may actually be a common-law employee if your employer controls the details on how the services are performed in these three key areas:

1. Behavioral (how, when, and where to perform the work).

2. Financial (extent of unreimbursed expenses; worker investment, profit or loss; payment terms).

3. Relationship (written contracts, benefits, employment time frame).

Why is this important? In a word—*taxes*. A W2 is considered an employee or statutory employee and the employer must withhold federal income tax. Also a W2 could be eligible for employer-provided benefits. An independent contractor, according to the IRS, is considered a 1099 based on the aforementioned description and is responsible for paying federal income taxes quarterly. If it's still unclear, employers can avoid paying hefty back taxes by filing IRS form SS-8, "Determination of Employee Work Status for Purposes of Federal Employment Taxes and Income Tax Withholding" with the IRS. The form lists approximately 20 questions that help to determine if you qualify as a W2 employee or a 1099 independent contractor/consultant. Visit *www.irs.gov/forms_pubs/ formpub.html* to obtain the document online in your choice of several file formats.

The technical independent contractor possesses the greatest exposure to potential IRS withholding issues. In fact, most high-tech employers will only hire consultants with W2 status to avoid potential IRS audits. Another reason for hiring W2s is that it costs companies far less to process invoices for your services through a few agencies as opposed to several thousand invoices from each individual consultant. When you consider that in some high-tech companies, 20 to 40 percent of the workforce is contingent, hiring W2s instead of 1099s can add up to substantial administrative savings.

Due to the nature of new high-tech and computer-related jobs, most of the assignments are project specific. Many projects vary in duration and some can be quite lengthy. Make certain you understand the IRS rules concerning the work relationship and ask prospective clients about any policies they might have concerning temporary workers.

According to Ron Lieber, in the article "The Permatemps Contretemps" (*Fast Company*), back in 1990, the IRS cited Microsoft for not withholding taxes from independent contractors employed by Microsoft for lengthy time periods. Microsoft was asked to change its policies to ensure that taxes were collected and had to aid contractors in paying back taxes. As a result, Microsoft established an arrangement with a local temporary employment agency and most contractors had to sign up with the agency, which became responsible for withholding taxes. Some independent contractors on long-term projects were hired full-time and others on shorter-term projects were retained as independent consultants. Recent policy limits the extent of a temporary contractor's employment to one year, after which the contractor must refrain from employment at Microsoft for a 100-day period.

As reported in *The New York Times on the Web* article "Microsoft Settles Suit With Temp Workers," several thousand so called "permatemps," who work as temps for one or more years, filed a class action lawsuit in 1992 alleging that Microsoft improperly denied them benefits. Eight years later, Microsoft agreed to pay a $97 million settlement.

If you're truly an independent contractor based on the IRS description, you'll need to pay quarterly estimated taxes based on your net income (income less expenses). Expect to receive a 1099 form from your client(s) toward the end of the year. We'll discuss the tax and financial implications of becoming a permanent temp later in the book.

How Does the IRS Determine a W2 From a 1099?

The IRS uses the following guidelines (paraphrased from IRS Form SS-8) to determine worker classification as W2 or 1099. The more control the employer exerts over the details of directing when, how, and where work is to be completed, the more likely it is that the employee falls into a W2 classification.

❖ What is the firm's business and what work will be done by the worker?

❖ Is the work done under a written agreement between the firm and the worker?

❖ Is the worker given training by the firm and is the worker given instructions in the way the work is to be done (exclusive of previously mentioned training)? Is the worker supervised or controlled during the performance of the service?

❖ Is the work for a particular job only or for an indefinite period of time and is the worker required to follow a routine or a schedule established by the firm? Does the worker provide a time record?

❖ What tools, equipment, supplies, and materials are furnished by the firm and the worker, and does the firm reimburse the worker for any expenses?

❖ Will the worker perform the work personally and does the work have helpers? Who hires and pays for the helpers?

❖ At what location are the services performed?

❖ What type of pay does the worker receive?

❖ Is the worker eligible for benefits (i.e. pension, bonus, paid vacations, sick pay, etc.)?

❖ How many hours a day does the worker perform service to the firm and does the worker perform similar services for others?

❖ Can the firm discharge the worker at any time without incurring a liability?

❖ Under what name does the worker perform services for the firm and does the worker advertise or represent himself or herself to the public as being in business to perform similar services? Does the worker have his or her own shop or office?

❖ Is a license necessary for the work?

❖ Does the worker have a financial investment in business related to the services performed?

❖ Can the worker incur a loss in the performance of the service for the firm?

❖ Has any other government agency ruled on the status of the firm's workers?

❖ Does the worker assemble or process a product at home or away from the firm's place of business and is the worker furnished with a pattern or given instruction to follow in making the product?

❖ Describe in detail any other reasons why you believe the worker is an employee or independent contractor.

❖ This section applies to salespeople or workers providing services directly to customers, and covers topics ranging from leads and pricing to territories and types of customers (for example, wholesale, retail, etc.).

For Whom Do I Really Work?

When you seek employment through an agency or agencies, you become an employee or W2 of the agency(ies) with whom you work. The agency is responsible for paying you and withholding the necessary income taxes. In the case of an independent contractor or free agent (not associated with any agency), you would be responsible for paying income tax on net income received. Remember, if you're not affiliated with an agency, regardless of what you're labeled (independent contractor or temp), it's the substance of the relationship that the IRS considers when determining whether the employer should withhold taxes.

Some employers, leery of possible IRS audits, are reluctant to hire independent contractors (1099s) directly. According to Dr. James R. Ziegler in *The Contract Employee's Handbook*, the result is that "pass-through agencies," or third party brokers, are sprouting to act on behalf of the independent contractor as a clearinghouse for collection, payment, and income tax withholding. The independent contractor retains the flexibility to set his or her own rates and bid directly on projects that specify contractors with W2 status because the broker becomes the "agency of record." There are a number of Web sites that act as brokers. For a small fee (usually 5 to 15 percent), they offer third party billing and tax withholding services.

Another option for the independent contractor is to incorporate; however, you may be subject to more up-front withholdings, and in some technical fields, this so called "corp to corp" status is still unacceptable. They prefer a third party arrangement. Discuss the details with an accountant or tax professional when deciding whether it's advantageous to incorporate.

The Pros and Cons of Temping

Outsourcing highly skilled and ready-to-work employees presents a competitive advantage by enhancing the speed at which today's high-tech, hypercompetitive organizations work.

In fact, many believe that organizational structure will continue to flatten and look more like the Figure 1.2 on page 24. What does this mean for temps? More opportunities to fully utilize your skills and gain a wider variety of organizational experience.

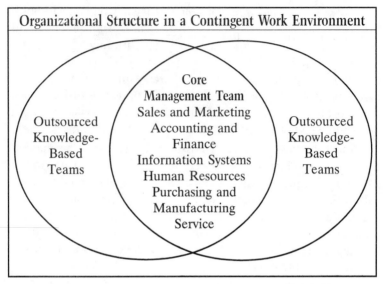

Organizational Structure in a Contingent Work Environment

Core
Management Team
Sales and Marketing
Accounting and
Finance
Information Systems
Human Resources
Purchasing and
Manufacturing
Service

Outsourced
Knowledge-
Based
Teams

Outsourced
Knowledge-
Based
Teams

Figure 1.2

Permanent temping provides:

❖ Job flexibility. Many assignments offer flexible work hours or the opportunity to work from a home office. For example, some help desk technicians are able to work an evening shift to keep their days free to attend college courses.

❖ Greater earnings potential. Several temps who work both independently and through an agency have reported earning more than when employed at a full-time job (*after paying for healthcare benefits!*).

❖ Increased productivity. Temping allows you focus on the project at hand without the distractions of being pulled away to work on other projects. Having a defined project helps avoid the "doing more with less" syndrome affecting so many companies today.

❖ Less corporate politics. Many temps agree that corporate politics have a much lesser effect on them than on their full-time counterparts. Without the political stress, these temps find their work more productive and enjoyable.

Temping as an interim solution provides:

❖ Increased potential for advancement. Temping allows you to gain the broad experience you need to advance your career without starting at the bottom.

❖ Opportunities for full-time work for professionals who are temping during a transition from one full-time position to the next. Both employer and employee can determine if the job is the right fit before investing time and money in training.

Now for the downside:

❖ Few, if any, healthcare or vacation benefits.

❖ Lack of a regular weekly paycheck or periods without any paycheck.

❖ Lack of stability—always starting over with each new assignment.

❖ Demands strong discipline and high motivation.

What Opportunities Are Available?

According to a May 17, 2000 press release found on *www.sireport.com*, the demand for professional services temps (finance, legal, scientific, marketing, etc.) is expected to experience the fastest revenue growth rate of 26 percent from 2000 to 2001 according to a Staffing Industry Associates report. According to an article in the *Monthly Labor Review*, the Bureau of Labor Statistics (BLS) cites a similar trend and anticipates the professional specialty group to grow by nearly five million workers by 2006. The BLS report also suggests an abundance of opportunity for the self-employed in fields such as computer science, math, writing, artistry, and healthcare. With technology playing a greater role in nearly every occupation, more extensive education and training requirements will increase.

To learn more about temporary job opportunities in your field, you can check your local newspapers. For a broader scope, the Internet is the best place to look. **A word of caution:** the volume of information can be overwhelming. There are millions of Web sites on jobs and tens of thousands of job boards. To get a general idea of opportunities in your field, try reviewing the opportunities listed on two or three job boards and recruiting sites. Also, go to a search engine and type "temporary employment agencies" or "job boards" and you'll receive a barrage of Web sites.

Another resource is to visit the Web sites of a few companies for which you'd like to work and view their career opportunities. You'll get an idea of the types of positions available, skills required, and the company philosophy. Although most positions may be full-time, in a tight labor market, companies might consider your proposal to work on an interim basis.

Finally, all major newspapers and many regional newspapers provide a searchable online classified database that connects to a national database. Start with the major newspapers like *The Wall Street Journal* or *The New York Times* online editions to identify what types of positions are in demand and the skills required.

Summary

Temping is more than simply bridging the gap between full-time jobs. It's a career lifestyle that spans a variety of functional areas and professional disciplines. While it has many advantages, you should take a realistic look at what permanent temping involves before embarking on the temporary lifestyle.

Key points:

❖ Temping can be an interim or continuous solution.

❖ Temping is a paradigm shift from "something to do in between jobs" to the future of the employment market in effectively allocating human capital to help companies quickly adapt to changing needs.

❖ The permanent temping lifestyle requires a certain amount of risk-taking, a strong commitment to taking control of your career, and an entrepreneurial spirit to locate and capitalize on business opportunities.

❖ The advantages of temping may not only be monetary, but also non-monetary in the form of flexibility and freedom to choose assignments.

❖ Temping can involve financial uncertainty due to the lack of a regular weekly paycheck and paid healthcare benefits.

❖ Know your status in the eyes of the IRS. W2 (You have an agency of record or are the employee of a company. In either case, taxes are being withheld); or 1099 (You are an independent contractor and bill your services directly to a variety of different clients and you pay the taxes directly through quarterly estimated payments or withhold them as an S Corporation).

Action Plan

It's time to start the planning process by answering the following questions. You may need to refer back to the previous questionnaire and job function chart.

1. Why are you interested in temping? (Possible responses could be to fill time while searching for a new job, to gain work experience while pursuing a new career or job function, or to obtain job flexibility.)

2. What job classification and function suits your skills and abilities? (Refer to the job function chart from this chapter.)

3. Take a skills inventory and make a list. Remember to include any special projects, team leadership roles, etc. and think in terms of key words that might be used in your profession or industry—they'll come in handy later when we discuss the hiring process in more detail. (*This would be a good time to dust off your resume. In Chapter 3 you'll be updating it.*)

4. Visit a few Web sites to get an idea of the amount of jobs available in your field and to determine the demand for your skills.

5. Check your local newspaper, a major national paper, or an online periodical for jobs in your field.

Making the Temporary Connection

Determined that you're interested in becoming permanent temp, it's time to connect with the opportunities that are right for you. In this chapter, we'll explore several ways to look for opportunities and the pros and cons of each method.

There are traditional and contemporary search methods. Your strategy should include a combination of the methods described. Traditional methods include: local newspapers, national newspapers (i.e. *The Wall Street Journal, The New York Times*, etc.), trade journals that specialize in your field, agencies in your area, and good old-fashioned networking. Contemporary methods are based on the Internet, such as: career portals, job boards, job search engines, online classifieds, industry-specific chat rooms and bulletin boards, e-zines, the online versions of brick and mortar agencies, and corporate recruiting sites.

With so much information available, locating the right opportunities is a job itself. That's why many busy professionals and those beginning a career as a permanent temp seek agency services to do the searching. When conducting your own Internet search, it's important to plan your strategy in order to avoid aimlessly wandering the vast array of digital information.

Agencies

A common search method is to sign with an agency specializing in temporary employment that will market you to potential clients. It's the easiest and fastest way to get started. Agencies negotiate your salary or hourly rate directly with the client based on pre-negotiated rates between you and the agency. You're paid by the agency directly—you become a W2 of the agency. You'll rarely know what the client is paying the agency for your services, but it will be a rate higher than what the agency is paying you, and the difference is the agency's fee or commission. The agency fee is typically a flat hourly fee such as $15 to $25, or 20 to 50 percent over pay rate based on what, if any, benefits are offered and accepted by you.

Agencies are structured in one of two ways:

1. Horizontal: agencies that run the full gamut of employment classifications for a variety of disciplines. For example, an agency that places people in a variety of positions such as clerical, technical, managerial, or executive is horizontal. Another example is an agency that places people with backgrounds in a variety of disciplines such as accounting and finance, sales and marketing, and light industrial. In other words, they place a variety of people in a variety of jobs.

2. Vertical: agencies specializing in a given employment classification or industry. For example, an agency specializing in all aspects of accounting from bookkeepers to CFOs is vertical. Another example is an agency that specializes in temporaries for the building and construction industry.

Some very large employment organizations such as Manpower, Adecco, Robert Half International (RHI), Management Recruiters International (MRI), and Spherion are hybrids of both horizontal and vertical because they have divisions specializing in both specific disciplines and job classifications. Other agencies are geographic-based when a major type of employment exists in a specific geographical area. For example, Silicon Valley and Silicon Alley are burgeoning with agencies specializing in technical talent.

Seek an agency that specializes in the placement of temporary or contract employees with your skills or job classification. For example, an executive should consider working with an agency specializing in the placement of interim executives. Another example would be a computer programmer specializing in C++ who would seek placement through a technical agency.

Freelance professionals generally encompass the creative realm, such as graphic artists, art directors, writers, voice talent, etc., and seek placement via specialized agencies or Web sites that attract bidders for creative talent. The work is usually based on a specific project for a fixed duration. Although some companies maintain a pool of freelance talent from which they draw on a regular basis, many freelance professionals also work independent of an agency. In this case, they market themselves directly to potential clients without the intermediary agency.

Contract workers run the gamut of professions and contract or guarantee their skill to a given employer for a fixed amount of time. The purpose can be project-related. For example, in the few years preceding the new millennium, many companies hired contract programmers specializing in COBOL programming language to update computer systems for Y2K readiness. There are agencies that specialize in contract professionals and provide the W2 status that many IT and computer-related positions require due to the lengthy duration and employer-employee relationship of these types of contract jobs. Generally referred to as consulting firms, independent contractors can also work on a 1099 basis.

For a list of staffing agencies by profession and work status, visit *www.staffing.com/directory.htm*. You may also consult Appendix A.

12 things to look for in a prospective agency

1. Are they experienced in placing temporary or contract professionals?

2. What is their industry specialty or placement niche? (For example, they may specialize in senior executives at the $150K and over salary range in the telecommunications industry.)

3. Who are their clients and do they have exclusive client relationships? (For example, some companies contract with an agency to outsource the staffing function. In this case, the only way into a specific company is via the contracted agency.)

4. How many years have they been in business?

5. How many counselors do they have and will you be assigned a single counselor?

6. How many placements have they made?

7. What benefits do they offer? What is their *written* policy regarding benefits?

8. Who pays the fee—client or employee?

9. What are the terms of the contract? (For example, are you free to also seek your own opportunities while working for an agency?)

10. For executive and high level technical positions, are there any legal non-disclosures, non-compete, or other restrictions that limit your scope of employment or ability to divulge information? (*You should check your employment record to make certain that you aren't currently under restrictions from any previous jobs, temporary or permanent.*)

11. What is the agency's turnaround time? (For example, once you sign on, how long does it take to find an assignment?)

12. Do they have the strategic relationships that will help you obtain the assignments and experience you desire?

Pros and cons of agencies

Working for an agency is a good way to start your permanent temporary career while establishing your own network. Other pros include:

❖ Agencies are proficient at locating opportunities in their already established networks.

❖ Good agencies will market your skills aggressively.

❖ Agency work helps you develop a network of your own more quickly than trying to locate the opportunities yourself.

❖ If you are an independent contractor, an agency can take on the burden of finding your next job while you continue working. You're able to focus on what you do best. The agency handles the marketing.

❖ Agencies allow you to work for clients that require W2 status by acting as your employer or agency of record to withhold taxes.

A good agency's reputation is based on the quality of its consultants, so if you're highly skilled, have excellent work ethics, and deliver the desired results, an agency will keep you working and clients will request you on subsequent projects.

A word of caution: If you wish to remain a permanent temp, avoid the employment trap. If you're good at what you do, you can easily become persuaded into becoming a permanent employee again.

Remember, however, that the agency's top priority is serving the corporate client. This can have a negative impact to the permanent temp in the following ways:

1. Negotiated rates may be lower than you could obtain on an independent basis.

2. You give up a certain amount of negotiating freedom in exchange for the agency's marketing, payroll, and tax withholding services.

When negotiating with your agency, know what your skills are worth in the open market. The amount of leverage you have with an agency depends on your skill level, the demand for your skills, and the size of the labor pool with similar skills. There are a number of Web sites that list the going rate for your skills. The Riley Guide compiled by Margaret F. Dikel, not only offers valuable salary comparisons, but also a comprehensive selection of career advice for job seekers. It's worth a visit to *www.dbm.com/jobguide* (dbm stands for Drake Beam Morin, a well-known career outplacement and counseling firm that hosts the Riley Guide). Another good salary site is *www.salary.com*. Select the "Salary Wizard" tab once you arrive at the site.

Other cons of going through an agency include:

❖ Lack of independence.

❖ Assignment to ill-suited jobs.

❖ Being sent on interviews as a sign of good faith for assignments which you have no chance of getting.

❖ Lack of regular assignments.

Finding the right agency

You can start by looking in your local newspaper or yellow pages under "employment," or you may also look under "career counseling" or "career placement." Look for agencies that list the most positions in your field. Using the local newspaper and yellow pages works well if you're looking for something close to home, or if you live in an area where there is an abundance of opportunity. As the parameters of your search expand (i.e. willing to commute or relocate), it makes sense to also seek large regional or national agencies via national newspapers or trade journals. Most of these publications have Web sites with an online help wanted section.

Most brick and mortar agencies have Web sites. You can search the Web by typing any of the following keywords into a search engine: "temporary employment agencies," "career placement agencies," "employment agencies," or "contract employment agencies." Many engineering, technical, and managerial positions can be found under the keyword "consulting agencies" or "independent consultants." Try using the same keywords on two or three search engines to yield varied results. You'll quickly see that the most popular agencies list in the top 10 or 20 on each search engine.

Finally, ask friends, associates, or other temps for advice on the best agencies.

Umbrella and pass-through agencies

Umbrella and pass-through agencies have begun to emerge in the technology sector, as the U.S. government has more vehemently investigated the use of a 1099 independent contractor classification. Many independent contractors may have been incorrectly classified as 1099s when, based on the IRS guidelines for determining employee classification, they are actually W2s making the companies for which they work responsible for tax withholding.

To avoid stiff tax penalties resulting from misclassification, more high-tech companies require W2 status and an agency of record as a condition for hiring independent contractors. Prior to umbrella and pass-through agencies, contractors were forced to sign on with agencies at agency-negotiated rates to have a third party collect the necessary withholding taxes and reduce the company's exposure to potential IRS audits and tax liabilities. Independent contractors had to give up a certain amount of freedom to negotiate their own arrangements.

The benefit of umbrella and pass-through agencies is that they allow independent contractors the ability to market themselves to and negotiate with potential clients while providing third party billing and W2 status required by many high-tech firms. The fees range from 5 to 15 percent to cover the costs associated with billing, collection, and tax withholding. Some offer optional fee-based services that can extend the total percentage beyond 15 percent.

An umbrella agency operates like a consulting firm establishing each independent contractor as a separate division. All divisions share the billing and collection services provided by the firm for a fee. Umbrella agencies also offer their members healthcare benefits and tax deferred retirement programs, among other benefits.

Pass-through agencies act as your agency of record and provide billing, collection, and tax withholding services. In addition, pass-throughs also provide healthcare benefits and tax deferred retirement programs. Some agencies will even offer sponsorship to TN (Trade Nafta) and H-1B Visa holders.

As with any agency there is a contract. However, unlike traditional agencies and brokers, umbrella and pass-through agency contracts usually do not include employment restrictions and non-compete clauses commonly found in traditional agency contracts.

Visit the following Web sites to learn more about umbrella and pass-through agencies:

❖ *www.Chancellor.com* (offers sponsorship and green card obtainment assistance for Canadian TN or H-1B Visa holders).

❖ *www.Ework.com* (offers a variety of billing and time tracking services along with benefits).

❖ *www.pacepros.com* (part of Dr. James R. Ziegler's Professional Association of Contract Employees, P.A.C.E., and author of the Contract Employees Handbook at *www.cehandbook.com*).

❖ *www.rmpcp.com* (RMP Consulting Partners, LLC specializing in computer and high-tech consulting).

Job Boards and Career Portals

Job opportunities proliferate the Internet in dedicated search sites, aggregate search sites, company search sites, and organization and association sites. According to a Forrester Research report, 32 percent of all recruitment advertising budgets will be spent on the Internet. The report also notes that four out of five companies post help-wanted ads on job boards and 54 percent post jobs on their company Web site. With so much information at your fingertips, the Internet can easily overwhelm you with information. This section will teach you how to search the Internet for job opportunities. I'll list the large and more popular career sites. The speed at which information changes on the Web is so rapid that a lengthy list of sites would be obsolete before I complete this chapter!

Job boards are searchable databases of jobs that allow you to sort by a variety of parameters such as keywords, occupation, skills, location, pay rate range, etc. Similar to the agency structure described earlier, some job boards are general and others are specific to an association, industry, or skill. Some focus on a particular industry with a variety of work arrangements, while others focus on a specific work arrangement in a variety of industries. There are also niche job boards that cater to very specific groups such as creative freelance professionals. Try typing *"freelance and contract job boards"* into one or more search engines. Your local area may also have several job boards that you can access by typing, *"contract jobs* and [*location*]" or *"temporary jobs* and [*location*]"* into one or more search engines.

Some popular job boards for freelance and contract work include:

❖ *www.ants.com.* A job bidding site for freelance professionals in a variety of industries.

❖ *www.bullhorn.com.* A job bidding site for freelance creative professionals.

❖ *www.careerbuilder.com.* Features a variety of industries and work arrangements, mega search lets your exclude specific companies from your search.

❖ *www.computerwork.com.* Features IT and high-tech positions in a variety of work arrangements.

❖ *www.dice.com.* Features IT and high-tech positions in a variety of work arrangements.

❖ *www.Ework.com*. Features a variety of industries specific to independents and includes optional fee-based services for independents.

❖ *www.freeagent.com*. Features a variety of industries specific to independents.

❖ *www.guru.com*. Features a variety of industries for independent professionals.

❖ *www.hotjobs.com*. Features a variety of industries and work arrangements (headhunters and staffing agencies are prohibited).

❖ *www.icplanet.com*. A job bidding site for freelance professionals in a variety of industries.

❖ *www.nettemps.com*. Features a variety of industries and work arrangements.

A career portal is a mega career site that not only offers job boards, but also connects you to many resources and online communities that share advice on a wide variety of topics related to job searching. You may have to join or register with the site in order to access all areas.

A few popular career portals include:

❖ *www.brassring.com*.

❖ *www.monster.com*.

❖ *www.myjobsearch.com*.

Many brick and mortar agencies also have Web sites. In fact, you'll find that the majority of listings on job boards are placed by employment agencies. If you plan to search independently and avoid using an agency, carefully screen jobs posted on job boards to make certain that they are listed directly by the hiring company and not an agency.

Finally, try general reference sites such as *www.about.com* (*jobsearch.about.com/careers/jobsearch/mbody.htm*) and *www.askjeeves.com* for assistance with your online job search.

One stop shopping

You're probably wondering that with all this technology, there's got to be a way to execute a simultaneous search of all online job boards. You're right! There are several meta job search engines that simultaneously search several job boards. Some provide auto responders that e-mail your search results based on a profile that you complete.

A few popular job search engines include:

❖ *www.careerbuilder.com.*

❖ *www.flipdog.com.*

❖ *www.freelanceworkexchange.com.* A conglomerate of many freelance and contract Web sites. You can register for free and receive a free report with links to the top 50 freelance Web sites.

❖ *www.job-search-engine.com.*

❖ *www.jobsleuth.com.*

Many of these sites contain full-time positions, so wherever possible, select *temporary, part-time,* or *contract* filters to better narrow your search results. Other terms to consider are *telecommuting, offsite job opportunities, alternative staffing, interim employment*, and *consulting.*

Careerxroads.com is the companion Web site to the book *CareerXroads* (MMC Group, 2000). Written by Gerry Crispin and Mark Mehler, it is an excellent reference book of over 500 job boards and job/career related sites. You can register at the Web site to receive regular updates to the book.

To specialize or not to specialize

There are different schools of thought on using specialty sites versus general employment sites. Specialty sites list opportunities specific to your field, whereas general employment sites list opportunities in your field among other fields. The advantage of visiting industry specific sites is that the search results will more closely match your specialty, saving you time in sorting through non-applicable jobs and fine-tuning your queries. The disadvantage is that they may yield less total jobs.

General employment sites may be considered too broad, even though they can be sorted by industry and job classification. However, many of the general sites have the marketing influence to attract the large volume of corporate clients to post their employment opportunities. On most sites, it costs you nothing but the time it takes to post your resume or complete a profile, so you really have nothing to lose by signing up with several sites.

Consider the strategy of a recruiter or human resources professional looking for someone with your skills. What tactics would they use to find the right candidates? Most would agree that they would consider specialty sites as well as the very large job boards. Select as many of the most popular general and specialty employment sites as time permits and post your qualifications.

Allow yourself plenty of time to evaluate them and determine the best sites for your skill specialty.

Pros and cons of job boards and career portals

The Internet contains a vast array of opportunities for permanent temps who know where to go to find the right opportunities. Develop an action plan for using the Internet to avoid becoming sidetracked and wandering aimlessly in cyberspace. The Internet provides key advantages for the permanent temp including:

❖ A wide variety of opportunities for finding work independent of an agency.

❖ A fast and easy method to search and respond to opportunities.

❖ Timesaving automatic search techniques that e-mail your results.

❖ Convenient searching 24 hours a day, seven days a week.

❖ Access to companies amenable to alternate work arrangements such as telecommuting, temporary, contract, and freelance.

Armed with a strategy, you'll find the Internet fast, convenient, and efficient at locating the right opportunities. Be prepared to complete an online profile to yield the job opportunities you seek, by knowing the work arrangement (i.e. temporary, contract, temporary to hire, etc.), the industry or field (i.e. finance, marketing, technical, etc.), and depending on the search engine, a variety of other parameters such as job location and self imposed restrictions on which companies can view your information.

Despite its many advantages, the Internet is not without its challenges for the permanent temp, including:

❖ Overwhelming amount of information. With over a million job related sites, it's difficult to determine the most effective sites in this overcrowded market.

❖ Many positions are offered by agencies reducing opportunities for independent contract work.

❖ Competition for positions is stiff—you become a "little fish in a big sea."

❖ Response is often slow or completely lacking. Many sites are deluged with such a large quantity of applicants that they have difficulty responding to the bottleneck of inquiries even with automated candidate management systems. As a result, many receive either a standard automated response or no response at all.

❖ Privacy and confidentiality are often limited or lacking. However, that's beginning to change as privacy laws mandate that users be made aware of how their personal information is being used.

Review the privacy policies of sites where you plan to leave your personal information. Understand if the information will be distributed to third parties or other agencies before parting with your information. Be especially wary of sites asking for personal references and understand how they will be used before including them.

Corporate recruiting sites and industry associations

Another element in your strategy should include visits to the sites of companies for whom you would like to work. Many companies are investing heavily in their recruiting sites as a primary source of seeking talent. Visiting these sites gives you an opportunity to learn about the company philosophy and determine if you would like to work there.

Complete with resume builders, these sites often contain sophisticated features to encourage talented individuals to leave their resumes. There are usually a larger number of full-time positions than contract or temporary. However, you may wish to leave your resume because they might consider a temporary consultant to fill the void while searching for a full-time candidate. Use your marketing skill to convince them to hire a consultant thereby avoiding the costs of hiring a full-time person when a consultant can do the job.

Although searching individual corporations' recruiting sites may take a little longer and yield fewer results, they're a good resource if you have a specific organization in mind. On the other hand, searching corporations' Web sites individually can be more efficient if you're looking for assignments within a specific industry and know the key companies within that industry.

Another online alternative is to visit the Web sites and newsletters or periodicals of professional associations. Many positions may be listed as full-time; however, in a tight labor market, companies may consider a long-term temporary during the interim search. Industry association sites also allow member job seekers to post ads or resumes.

If you belong to an industry association, check their Web site for opportunities. To search for an industry association, type keywords relevant to the discipline such as *"engineering associations"* or *"engineering professional associations."* You can also substitute the *"society"* for *"association."*

Some of the larger industry associations have extensive job and career placement sections within their Web sites, making it worth your while to include them in your search. However, if you visit an industry association with job postings that are several months old, it's probably not time-effective to include them in your search strategy.

Company research sites

There are a number of company databases that provide more candid comments on companies without going to their specific site. Use these sites to learn more about a specific company for which you'd like to work. A good place to start is at Hoovers Online (*www.hoovers.com*). It provides corporate information along with information on industry competitors. For a more avant-garde site try *www.vault.com*.

Summary

In today's job market, there are numerous sources of job and career information. It's important to know what's available to you so that you can put together an integrated approach to reaping more permanent temping opportunities. With such an overwhelming amount of information, it's best to create a plan and allow yourself plenty of time and patience to connect with the right opportunities.

Key points:

❖ Integrate several sources in your search strategy, such as agency, Web searches, and corporate recruiting sites.

❖ Carefully read the terms of any agency contract to make certain there are no unwanted or excessive restrictions on your ability to continue your independent business.

❖ Have a Web strategy before you begin searching job boards and career portals.

❖ Carefully review recruiting sites' privacy policies before leaving your information, especially sites asking for references up front.

❖   Give yourself plenty of time to research opportunities via the Internet. It's easy to spend one workweek visiting and/or registering with employment sites.

Action Plan

Based on the information in Chapter 2, use the following action plan to connect with the right opportunities.

1. Based on your specialty and desired work arrangement, select a few agencies and contact those with which you would consider working.

2. Visit a few Web sites and, based on your specialty and desired work arrangement, select two or three recruiting sites. Analyze the pros and cons of these sites to determine those that work best for the type of search results you desire.

3. List any industry associations to which you belong or that you could target for opportunities or referrals.

4. Visit the sites of corporations for which you'd like to work and locate the available opportunities.

5. Set up a profile on a meta job search site, such as *flipdog.com* or a similar site, to begin receiving e-mail notifications of jobs in your field.

6. If you're a technical professional planning to go the independent contractor route, visit a few pass-through and umbrella agency sites so you're prepared when your client asks for your "agency of record."

7. Before you begin signing on to the various sites, read the next chapter to prepare yourself for the next step.

The Hiring Process

This chapter is designed to help you prepare what you'll need to get through the hiring process. Although there are differences between the online and offline hiring processes, both require a resume.

Preparing Your Resume

Now would be an appropriate time to update an old or current resume to make it more conducive to today's scanning and searching technologies. In today's business environment it is important to create several resumes that target specific job functions or classifications within your major area of interest. Additionally, you'll need a hard copy version for faxing or mailing along with an electronic version in ASCII text (.txt file format) or html (.htm or html format) for submitting your resume electronically. Your electronic resume will come in handy when completing online profiles and project bids.

Decide what type of resume best showcases your experience, accomplishments, and education. According to *jobstar.org*, the most popular formats are curriculum vitea (C.V.), chronological, and functional.

Use the C.V. style if you're an educator or scientist with many years of experience and a wide variety of projects, publications, and accolades. It will itemize each career step; cite publications, presentations, and education.

The chronological style is one of the most widely accepted styles. If you have a broad base of experience demonstrating a logical career progression with several similar companies, the chronological style is most effective. It includes your job history in reverse chronological order starting with the most current job. Within each job, it briefly describes your responsibilities.

The functional resume is ideal for individuals seeking to highlight accomplishments and focuses on the overall benefits of your skills and achievements. This resume uses bullets of functional categories such as "new business development," "operations management," and "project management," and provides the benefits of what you've accomplished. You'll still need to include the names of employers and dates of employment.

Scannable versus keyword searchable

It's important to distinguish between a scannable and keyword searchable resume. According to Rebecca Smith's eResumes & Resources (*www.eresumes.com*), scannable resumes are simply formatted, legible resumes that scan accurately into a resume databank or automated applicant-tracking system. The purpose of a scannable resume is to ensure accurate scanning by giving attention to the mechanics of formatting. Mechanics include wide margins; sans serif fonts, specific font sizes, paper size and color; and avoidance of graphic treatments such as lines, shaded boxes, etc.

A keyword resume (which can also be scannable) is one that includes keywords and phrases to describe job functions and achievements that are searchable by Internet job search engines and job matching services. Keywords and keyword phrases are commonly used industry jargon that demonstrates your skills for a specific job field. This format is especially useful when creating your resume in an html file format because it increases the number of hits you'll receive once your resume is posted. It's also useful in hardcopy resumes because recruiters often visually scan the resume looking for keywords and phrases.

When creating your resume, think in terms of key words and descriptive words related to the keyword especially if you are planning to post your resume to online job boards. Many career-related and contract employment sites offer sophisticated matching services. Such services scan your resume to determine a match between keywords on your resume and those listed in job descriptions. The search results return a list of jobs that more closely meet your specific skills. Keyword nouns are usually more identifiable to automated systems than action verbs.

For example, the resume for a corporate trainer would use the following descriptors: platform, program development, pre testing, post testing, and employment screening.

Consider the terms frequently used in your field and include them in your resume.

For example, a marketing vice president would include terms such as market segmentation, market analysis, e-commerce site launch, channel management, increased market share, brand management, etc.

If you're in the technical or computer sciences field, you would include terms such as UNIX platform, Java programming, virtual private network (VPN), peer-to-peer networks, proxy server setup, client-server setup, etc.

Including keywords increases the accuracy of a match that is consistent with your skills. When setting up profiles or search agents on Internet job searching sites, effective use of keywords will yield jobs that more closely match your skills and areas of interest. Keywords save time in sorting through search results because they ensure more relevant results. Agencies use keywords to help find the best match manually. In addition, keywords aid in moving your resume to the top of the pile, because they strongly indicate your range of experience and exude a level of expertise.

Resume file formats

ASCII text file format is the most universally acceptable. It's not the prettiest resume, but it's more functional and easily read by most word processing software. It's important to be sensitive to the file format required by the Web site. Most will accept resumes created in the more popular word processing software formats such as Word and WordPerfect. Many sites automatically convert your resume to ASCII and filter any graphics. In today's sophisticate Web sites, the conversion process is transparent to the end user.

ASCII formatted resumes can be sent as file attachments or cut and pasted into the body of an e-mail message. You'll see the benefit of cutting and pasting from your resume later when we discuss completing online profiles and agency applications.

Resumes that sell

Most experts agree that a resume should be a one- to two-page synopsis of your career accomplishments. But a resume is also your personal billboard, and like most billboards, it needs to sell the product or service in a clear, concise, and compelling manner. You must stress the benefits. Translate your skills into features that a prospective employer would recognize as a benefit. Read the following statements and determine which candidate is more appealing.

Candidate A: Managed the implementation of a corporate Web site.

Candidate B: Skilled project manager of a multinational team of developers launching a new Web site within three months.

Notice how candidate B includes keywords such as Web site, project management, and team. Candidate B not only tells what he did, but also mentions the expediency benefit of completing the project in three months.

It's important to differentiate yourself from every other candidate by showing measurable proof of your achievements. This is especially true for managerial and executive level positions. Show quantifiable results of your efforts. For example: increased profits by X percent; created an employee benefits Intranet, saving the company X dollars over a one year period; implemented a job training program that reduced accidents by X percent and reduced workers compensation claims by X percent. Look for ways to describe your career accomplishments in addition to the benefits they provide.

Qualify the scope of your responsibilities. If you're an executive responsible for several divisions, define the size and scope of those divisions and your accomplishments. For example: led three multinational divisions to profitability within six months, or increased operating profit by 12 percent in three $50 million divisions.

Providing measurable proof of your accomplishments will help set your resume apart from thousands of others and increase your response rate.

Do's and don'ts of resume writing

Do...

❖ Include keywords pertinent to your industry and job field.

❖ Include measurable proof of achievements, especially at the managerial and executive levels.

❖ Include certifications, training, and additional education relevant to the type of job you're seeking.

❖ List software programs, operating systems, and programming languages of which you have working knowledge or extensive experience.

❖ Include a qualifications summary that describes your experience and states the benefits of what you can do for a prospective employer. In the advertising business, this is referred to as the "hook" that draws readers in and entices them to want to continue reading. It's also the hook that makes them want to meet you. For example: "Over 15 years' experience in fund management for companies responsible for portfolios in excess of $50 billion." "Extensive e-commerce experience through designing the infrastructure, hiring teams, and managing the overall program."

❖ Include a cover letter—even with electronically submitted resumes.

❖ Proofread your resume and have another detail-oriented individual proofread it as well.

Don't...

❖ Lie, embellish, or otherwise "stretch the truth." Honesty is always the best policy for resume writing.

❖ Waste words describing what is understood by the job title. Sell the benefits of what you accomplished while performing the tasks associated with the job function.

❖ List an objective or become too specific in your summary introduction. Remember, the resume is designed to open doors.

❖ Offer references without understanding how they will be used and without a privacy guarantee. This is especially important when registering with employment or job bidding Web sites.

❖ Waste space with the phrase "references available upon request." If a prospective employer requires references, they'll ask for them.

❖ Send a resume without a cover letter even if a cover letter wasn't requested.

Cover letters

The cover letter is an essential companion to the resume and provides an opportunity to tailor your reply to a specific opportunity. The cover letter provides another opportunity to sell the benefits of contracting with you. Include a cover letter on all resumes, including those sent electronically, regardless of whether or not it was requested. Many job boards and career-related Web sites also offer an area where you can create one or more cover letter.

The cover letter should open by mentioning the position, source where the position was found, and a general, yet powerful statement about how you fit the position.

For example: "Your posting for a telecommunications media relations consultant on *prpros.com* reads like my resume. I'm an experienced public relations professional who has increased the media exposure of several key telecommunications clients two-fold." Or: "I'm enthused about the prospects of working with another e-commerce client noted in your posting on *hotprogrammers.com*. I'm a Web developer whose CGI scripts ensured fast, accurate order processing of over one million orders per day for a major Internet retailer.

This first paragraph should "hook" the reader and entice him to read on. Subsequent paragraphs highlight your achievements and convince the employer that you're the perfect candidate for the job. Include bulleted lists if necessary to emphasize your accomplishments and make them easier to read and retain. Remember to include the skills and traits specifically listed in the job description to increase your chances of consideration for the job.

Try to include information about the company to show you've taken an interest in them. For example, "ABC Corporation is well-known among engineering professionals for its cutting edge designs, and I've spent the past 5 years utilizing the latest design technology on the following projects:"

Close your cover letter by requesting an interview and letting the employer know how to reach you. Mentioning that you will contact the employer at a specific time is a proactive measure that demonstrates good follow-up skills.

There are a lot of good books and Web sites on the details of effective resumes and cover letters. Many of these sites provide fee-based resume writing services. Look for additional resume tips by typing "resume writing tips" into a search engine. Typing the word "resume" alone will yield well over one million sites, including resume banks. Also search the career portals and job board sites listed in Chapter 2, as they contain helpful tips on resume writing.

A few good Web sites on resume writing and cover letters include:

❖ *www.eresumes.com.*

❖ *www.resumania.com.*

There are hundreds of books on writing resumes and cover letters. Some even specialize in specific types of resumes and job classifications. The following books will get you started:

❖ *101 Great Resumes* by the editors of publisher, Career Press.

❖ *Building a Great Resume* by Kate Wendleton.

❖ *America's Top Resumes for America's Top Jobs: A Complete Career Handbook* by J. Michael Farr.

❖ *Resumes for Dummies* by Joyce Lain Kennedy.

❖ *Cover Letters for Dummies* by Joyce Lain Kennedy.

❖ *Cover Letters! Cover Letters! Cover Letters!* by Richard Fein.

The Agency Interview

If you opt to seek contract and temporary employment through an agency, you'll be interviewed, and in some cases, screened for the aptitude and/or skills necessary for the types of positions you seek. The agency interview is a general assessment of your skills and overall marketability. Depending on the type of position, you may be asked to take a test. Tests can measure your aptitude at a specific skill, screen to validate that you can do what you say you can, or develop a psychological profile of your suitability for various job types.

What is the agency looking for?

Aside from a neat appearance and professional demeanor, agencies are looking for specific industry expertise and knowledge, and above all, your ability to articulate your knowledge and expertise. You must exhibit clear, concise communication skills and the ability to express yourself with a well-targeted presentation. Many people are almost embarrassed to sell themselves and depend too heavily on the resume to do the selling, while others go off on a lengthy soliloquy that really says nothing.

You have approximately two minutes after the initial icebreakers to open the door and make an impression that sets the tone for the next 45 minutes to an hour. Interviewing is an art and must be practiced and rehearsed. An interview is a dialog where you need to guide the interviewer at the appropriate time to ask questions about your strengths.

Silence is an effective interviewing technique. If you have nothing to say, maintain eye contact and either say nothing or ask, "Do you have any other questions?"

The interviewer generally asks three levels of questions:

1. Need to know (questions that are relevant to the job).

2. Nice to know (questions that, when answered, would help the interviewer account for certain potential situations).

3. Curious to know (questions that might indicate an applicant's social fit within the organization).

Be prepared to answer questions about information that is "nice to know" or that the interviewer is "curious to know." Legally, an interviewer cannot directly ask for this information, such as, "Do you have children?" or "Are you married?" For example, an interviewer trying to determine if a woman has children that might prevent her from arriving at work early for international video teleconference meetings might say, "This job involves regular early morning video teleconferences with their Japanese affiliate. Do you see this as a problem?" Your reply could be, "Although I have certain commitments, I can make alternative arrangements, so I don't see this as a problem."

Connecting on a personal level with the interviewer is almost as important as your accomplishments. Look for ways in which you may be able to establish this connection. For example, if you notice the interviewer has a plaque for running in a local marathon, you might say, "I see you're a runner. I also ran in that marathon." Or if there's a diploma from a school from which you also attended, you might say, "I see you're an ABC University graduate. I also graduated from ABC University, from their business school."

If you've spent a number of years in a traditional industry or have breadth of experience in new and emerging industries, you possess a highly marketable skill that cannot be easily learned. How well do you articulate what you know? Refer back to the job function chart in Chapter 1 to review the traits of each function. This provides additional insight into what an agency is looking for. Depending on your job function (executive, knowledge-based, implementer), your industry and job specialty knowledge are equally as important as skills proficiency.

An executive needs to exude a sense of leadership and possess extensive industry knowledge, including measurable proof of accomplishments. For example, an executive with extensive experience in new media should articulate knowledge of the industry, including trends. Leadership can be demonstrated in the accomplishments that helped influence the industry or induce a company's growth. Board level and committee chair positions with industry associations also demonstrate leadership and show commitment to the industry.

The knowledge-based worker must demonstrate a strong proficiency in his/her specialty area. For example, an IT technology specialist with extensive background in computer networks should articulate a macro knowledge of networks from both a hardware and a software perspective. Knowledge should include current technology and imminent technological advances. Participation in industry associations and involvement with academic institutions are a few ways to demonstrate your commitment to the profession.

A technician needs to prove s/he has the skills and proficiency to perform specific tasks. For example, a marketing manager experienced in new product launches would emphasize project management skills. Describing the launch strategy and emphasizing the return on investment demonstrates proficiency.

In any case, prepare a personal deliverables statement that sums up your experience, highlights your key strength, and stresses the benefit of hiring you. A personal deliverables statement helps you answer the question "Tell me about yourself." For example, "I'm a financial analyst specializing in obtaining venture capital for pre-IPO biotech companies. The majority of my projects received third and fourth round financing and several went public within a four to six month period."

Notice how the deliverables statement tells you who this person is (financial analyst), what they do (key strength in obtaining venture capital), and an important benefit (obtains funding frequently and goes public quickly). The personal deliverables statement makes it easier for the agency to market you to potential clients. It will also come in handy later when we discuss networking and for completing online applications on contract and freelance Web sites.

The Client Interview

The client is trying to ascertain how well you'll fit within their organization in addition to your level of proficiency for the position. Organizational fit relates to your personality type and how well you'll adapt to the organization's culture.

For example, a company that has recently undergone an IPO and now seeks to roll out a new high-tech product will need a savvy marketing professional experienced in working with technical people, and who has the wherewithal to work effectively in the energetic, often chaotic environment following an IPO.

If you and your agency have done your homework, you'll be aware of the situation and tailor your comments and deliverables statement to address the situation. Think of the agency interview as a dress rehearsal for the client interview except that the client will consider how well you fit the specific organization, as opposed to the agency's view on how marketable you are to a number of organizations.

Distance interviews

With today's flexible work force and high-tech communications tools, you may be interviewed from a remote location via a video teleconference. This holds true if the position is for an offsite telecommuter. In this case, you'll be asked to go to a local center (i.e. company branch office, hotel, Kinkos, etc.) to attend the video teleconference.

Although it may seem a bit more intimidating than the typical face-to-face interview, relax and be yourself. Think of it as just another video teleconference except, instead of keeping a job, you're vying for one. Practice in front of a mirror or videotape yourself to help feel more comfortable during the actual interview.

The interview may also be conducted via voice teleconference as a pre-screening before deciding whether to fly you to headquarters for an in-person interview. It's important to speak clearly and let your personality come through without dominating the conversation. Avoid the use of slang or colloquialism especially when interviewing with a multinational corporation, as the interviewer may not be of the same nationality. For example, when responding to the question, "How are you today?" you wouldn't reply with, "I'm finer than a hair on a frog split two-ways." Enough said.

Preparing for the interview

Preparedness is the key to successful interviewing. With the abundance of easily obtainable corporate information, companies today *expect* that you'll arrive at the interview well-informed. In addition to knowing about the company for which you're interviewing, as the great philosopher Socrates once said, "Know thyself." This advice couldn't be more prudent than in the context of a job interview. Know all the names, dates, numbers, and responsibilities covering past jobs. Be prepared to talk about your strengths *and* weaknesses.

Relate your strengths and accomplishments directly to the job for which you're interviewing. Weave them into the context of the conversation where possible. For example, the interviewer mentioned that she likes to arrive early to get a cup of coffee and compose herself before beginning the day. You might respond, "I found that being an early bird not only helps me better plan and organize my day, but also affords me a little extra time to scan trade journals and stay current with best practices in my industry." In the example, what could have been misinterpreted as small talk by the candidate, was turned into an opportunity to interject several strengths.

When talking about your weaknesses, remember to put a positive spin on them. For example, you disliked your last boss because he micromanaged you. Rephrase it by saying, "While I thrive in an independent work environment, free to be creative, I learned a lot about management by working with my former manager, who had a more controlling management style." Prepare to discuss your weaknesses in advance. Think about any mistakes you've made and why. Determine what you learned from them and how you could have avoided them or prevented them from reoccurring.

According to Ron Fry, author of *101 Great Answers to the Toughest Interview Questions*, interviewers are looking for confidence, enthusiasm, experience, and dependability. "The better you know yourself, the better you can sell yourself to a prospective employer when you're on the spot in an interview."

Consider the following when preparing for the interview:

❖ Research the company and have an idea of what they do, their size in revenue, number of offices, and amount of people. (Hint: visit their Web site and look at the last paragraph of recent press releases. It usually sums up the company in a concise statement.) Include any recent news about the company along with product and financial information. It's a good idea to know who their competitors are in a given field. Visit *www.hoovers.com* (select "Companies and Industries" button) for basic information regarding a company's competitive landscape.

❖ Jot down a few ways in which your skills and experience could benefit this company—remember your personal deliverables statement.

❖ Look for any connections between your experience and the company. For example, say the company has an office in London and you helped open a regional sales office for a previous company in London. Make the connection clear during the interview. Some connections make good icebreakers or can be easily worked into the conversation.

❖ Prepare a list of questions that you have regarding the company for which you're interviewing. Your questions should be asked within the scope and flow of the interview. Remember the interview is a dialog and your questions demonstrate your interest in the company. The questions should be relevant to the position and its influence on the company—not, "how long are breaks?" or "do you have a smoking lounge?" Asking questions is a sign of interest in the company. Typical questions can include:

❖ To whom does this position report?

❖ Are there other consultants in this department?

❖ Would I interface with other consultants or departments, and if so, who will they be?

❖ What specific results are you looking for and what bottom line impact will those results have?

❖ How will you evaluate the results?

❖ Please describe the corporate culture and management philosophy.

❖ If your research has uncovered interesting news on the company, now would be a good time to ask. For example, you've read that the company recently merged with a competitor. You should ask if the merger would affect the project on which you'll work. (Note: if you're an executive who's been hired to facilitate the post merger transition, this would not be a good question.)

❖ Bring a few extra copies of your resume in paper form and on diskettes along with references and, if applicable, your portfolio.

The following book provides a systematic approach to helping you prepare for even the most demanding interview: *101 Great Answers to the Toughest Interview Questions 4th Edition* by Ron Fry.

What should I wear?

In today's casual offices it's often tempting to dress casually for an interview. Because those first few seconds of an interview usually make the most profound impression, err on the side of caution and dress conservatively in a suit for women and suit and tie for men. The same advice holds true for jewelry. Men should remove earrings and women should refrain from bulky, pretentious jewelry that can become distracting. Be a radio, where they listen to your words, not a television, where they're distracted by your image.

The Online Hiring Process

Job bidding or auction sites operate with sophisticated matching algorithms that sort and filter candidates based on a number of parameters that you set when completing a profile. A profile is basically your resume in the format supplied by the Web site. There's usually a place to paste your existing resume in either text or html format. The profile is usually the first step in the process of becoming a member of the site and its database of temporary professionals. Have your resume and, if applicable, electronic portfolio samples handy when completing these forms.

Most sites provide the option of receiving e-mail alerts when new jobs are posted that match your profile. There's a science involved in creating a profile that gets accurate matches. If you find that you're not getting suitable results or the volume that you had anticipated, review your profile selections. The help systems and FAQ sections are usually quite clear, but if you're still having difficulty, contact support. They're usually responsive and eager to help ensure your online success.

Job bidding sites usually charge the client a fee for posting contract and temporary job openings. They also charge bidders a small fee of 5 to 10 percent of the total project bid once the bid is accepted. You're paid directly by the company operating the Web site, less the fee, and they collect the total from the client. All correspondence is conducted via the Web site and most sites offer a variety of additional free and fee-based services, such as billing and collection and project management application software.

Your IRS work status varies with each site. Some are simply intermediaries connecting clients with professionals and vice versa for a small percentage fee. In this case, you're a 1099 and responsible for paying taxes. A few of the high-tech specialty sites offer W2 status while others allow you to remain a 1099. Some sites provide the option on an as-needed basis. For example, a company that posts a contract position may specify W2s only. In this case, you'll evoke your W2 status and allow the Web site to withhold taxes so that you can bid on the project. Check the Web site's policies to understand if there is a fee for this service.

Take the time to read and understand the sites' policies and any fees associated with creating a profile. Most sites do not charge you to have a profile, but there are a few that allow you to have one free profile and charge for subsequent profiles. You may also be required to refresh your profile every so often. It's in your best interest, as well as the site's, to keep your profile accurate and up-to-date. Some sites also offer "premium" jobs for members only and charge a monthly fee to be considered for such opportunities.

The forms are easy to complete and the user interfaces vary in complexity among the different online sites. Most sites provide step-by-step instructions to assist with completing the forms. Aside from the usual name, address, etc., there are comment boxes where you'll describe yourself and your area(s) of specialty. This is another good place to include your personal deliverables statement. The other selections are simple drop down boxes for things such as occupation, area of specialty, type of work arrangement, years of experience, certifications, etc.

Choose a reliable group of effective and trustworthy agents and Web sites. Signing up with employment sites can be a tedious and time-consuming process, so narrow your selection down to the sites that best suit your skills. You'll want to allow yourself at least 45 minutes to an hour to complete the online form. If you're a creative professional such as a designer, you'll need an electronic portfolio. Sites specializing in creative talent recommend and some even require portfolio samples, which you'll upload to their site.

When you receive e-mail notification that a job matches your profile or during a search of job postings, you find a suitable job, place your bid on the job. If required, attach samples or other information requested by the company posting the job. Most sites offer a selection to contact the client directly if you have any questions. There is also an area where you can add comments, which is a good location for your cover letter.

Chapter 2 advised you to use caution before leaving your references on Web sites, but it bears mentioning again. Understand how and for what purpose references will be used before including them in your profile. Know the sites' privacy policies and whether or not information contained within your profile is made available for sale or otherwise to third parties. When in doubt... don't!

Summary

A good deal of preparation is involved before you even begin looking for temporary opportunities. Take the time up front to create a resume and cover letter that really sell your skills and accomplishments. Also, spend time preparing for each interview so that you're poised, cool, and confident. As mentioned earlier, the process of looking for a job is a job in itself. However, if you plan your strategy and integrate several methods of job searching, you're on your way to a successful temping career.

Key Points

❖ Update your resume with clarity and keywords to optimize the use of today's scanning and searching technologies.

❖ Select a style that accentuates your best attributes.

❖ Include a cover letter with every resume, including those sent electronically.

❖ Develop a personal deliverables statement that briefly and concisely tells who you are, what you do, and the key benefit of hiring you.

❖ Prepare for the interview by researching the company and tailor your responses to suit the needs of the company.

❖ Carefully review the policies and fees associated with becoming a member of an online job bidding or contract employment Web site.

❖ Post your profile on sites that best suit your skills and take the time to complete each profile accurately.

Action Plan

At this point, some of you may have a lot of work to do. Don't despair. Spending up-front time to hone your resume, perfect your interviewing techniques, and complete a few online profiles will pay off in the long run.

1. Begin by reviewing your resume. Set a date to complete the review and update. Remember, if you need an objective third party, hire a professional resume writer to get to off to a good start.

2. Develop a personal mission statement that is realistic and achievable. It should represent your personal timeline for establishing the necessary contacts to land the contracting jobs that you believe will best utilize your skills. For example: "Establish a consulting practice that will result in assignments that will run six months to one year in duration in the new media field."

3. Review your experience, skills, and accomplishments and develop your personal deliverables statement. Use it in your cover letter template.

4. Develop a cover letter template that contains three to four paragraphs that can easily be customized for a variety of positions.

5. Proofread your resume and cover letter for any errors. It's always best to have another person review it. You'll be surprised at some of the things you overlook when trying to proof your own work.

6. Once your resume and cover letter are finished, you're ready to complete a few online profiles for which you'll need the information from your resume and cover letter.

7. Search the Web or purchase a book on interviewing tactics. It will help you anticipate common interviewing questions and better prepare to answer them.

8. As silly as it may feel, rehearse your interview in front of a mirror or record it, then critique yourself. The more you rehearse, the more natural it will become. Start by rehearsing your personal deliverables statement.

9. Develop a list of standard questions that you should ask during the interview.

Compensation

You're probably wondering what type of compensation packages are available, who pays you, and how much leverage you really have. As with all commodities... it depends. Supply and demand have a large impact on your rate as does you skill proficiency and experience level.

Types of Compensation

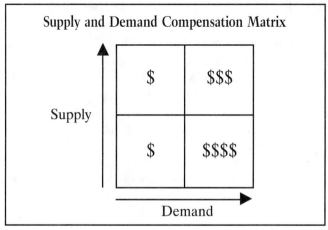

Figure 4.1

Let's take a look at the types of compensation available relative to various organizational levels, professional disciplines, and your level of experience.

Hourly rate

Most positions outside of executive and managerial are paid on an hourly rate basis. The rate varies based on the types of skills, the demand for those skills, and the labor supply available. Hourly rate temps at the "preprofessional level," such as clerical, would also be eligible for time and a half pay. Professionals, mid-level managers, and technical consultants (non-executive) compensated on an hourly rate should establish a straight time overtime rate in addition to straight time.

Executives are compensated based on a professional day (pro day) as opposed to an hourly rate. A pro day rate remains the same regardless of hours, and executives are exempt from overtime pay.

Whether you're an independent contractor (1099) or an employee of an agency (W2), hourly rates are the most commonly used form of compensation in the temporary and independent contractor fields. In addition to hourly rates, freelance and independent contractor Web sites usually provide several other options for bidding on projects such as per project rate or a combination of project rate and hourly rate for time over and above estimated project duration.

An hourly rate allows clients to easily budget project work, better plan resource loading, and accurately control project costs. Hourly rates are also easier to track for rate comparisons.

If you sign with an agency, you'll negotiate an hourly rate that's based on the market hourly rate for your skills. The table on page 73 provides estimates based on full-time employees. Another way to estimate your hourly rate is to divide the salary for the same full-time position by 1,000. The result may be a little higher than what the agency will offer. However, it will be a good figure to use if you're quoting the job as an independent contractor because it includes the amount for benefits, which you'll have to obtain if you're independent, or if your agency doesn't provide them.

Hourly rates for independent contractors are higher than their agency temping counterparts and the difference represents the benefits and the agency commission. To remain competitive and in the best interest of the client, agency rates are established to provide the best talent at a fair market price that benefits all parties involved. In addition, the rates must allow for the agency markup. The agency markup includes the costs associated with marketing you to potential clients and providing the billing and collection service that you would otherwise be responsible for as an independent consultant. We'll discuss more about the financial aspects of being an independent consultant in a later chapter.

Per project

Per project fees are commonly found in the freelance creative area and often there is a written fee schedule to give clients a general idea of how much something will cost. Of course, the fee schedule is not a substitute for a detailed price proposal. Projects are priced within a range for a proposed assignment. The range you determine for specific projects is based on a number of variables:

1. Years of experience.

2. Level of knowledge.

3. Prevailing market rate.

4. Prestige of your existing clientele as well as your own "credibility quotient." For example, if you were the principle designer for several major Fortune 500 Web sites, then you could command a higher project fee for your services than a designer for a small local business.

5. The severity of the client's dilemma. (How deep is the pain that the client is experiencing?) For example, hiring a successful temporary lawyer specializing in contract law at a premium price is far less than the potential payout from losing a multimillion-dollar lawsuit.

The project fee is helpful when the full scope of a project is uncertain. For example, you have an idea of what it will take, but the client isn't quite clear and may decide to make a few changes mid-project. In this case, you'll have a little cushion if the project goes beyond the duration you had anticipated, plus it covers your time for client revisions. To control project changes that may impact net earnings, carefully negotiate the contract. You'll need to clearly define project deliverables and the consequences of not delivering. A common practice is to charge a project fee and a reduced per diem rate for time over and above the original project estimate, resulting from specification creep or overall change in project scope and/or goals.

Per diem

Per diem is a rate method commonly found in the healthcare, education, and business analyst professions. However, consultants also use it, especially when the project requires local commuting or other distance travel. Per diem is generally used when the work performed is clear and understood. For example, in the case of a pediatric nurse, the duties performed are fairly standardized across the profession, as are the rates. A per diem worker is usually compensated for travel time, mileage, food, and other miscellaneous expenses associated with getting to and from the job on a daily basis.

A word of caution here—check with your agency or client to determine the rates allowed for lodging and meals and incidental expenses (M & IE). IRS publication 1542 specifies maximum rates without considering per diem allowances as part of wages for tax purposes. There are two methods described in the publication. One is determined by the locality to provide a greater allowance for a more expensive metropolitan area versus a lesser expensive rural area. The second method is the standard federal rate.

What's the best method to use hourly versus per project?

The best method depends on the situation, scope of the job, and common industry practice. Savvy clients have an idea of what the market value is for your skills before speaking with you. Using a per project fee is effective when you have enough experience in your area of expertise to know the time and effort involved in producing what the client requests, and if it is a widely accepted practice in your industry. Most per project fees will allow a cushion to ensure your profitability if changes are made during the project or if the project extends slightly beyond the anticipated duration.

If you're uncertain about the total scope of the project or the client isn't clear on the expectations and outcome, the hourly rate may be a safer method, although you'll still need to have an estimate of the total duration. There's no substitute for clearly defined project goals, objectives, milestones, and completion dates. If the client doesn't provide this, you need to draft something for the client's approval.

Remember to include time and materials as part of the compensation package, and specify who supplies the tools required to do the job and who owns the end result. Materials could include any equipment, machinery, supplies, etc.

Temp to hire

While this book is about professional temping, situations may arise that could (if mutually desired) result in a full-time position. Temp to hire is the human resources equivalent of "try before you buy." It doesn't really affect your compensation while you're employed with the agency; however, the client may decide to buy out your contract and offer you a full-time position at a different hourly rate. Hopefully, if they decide to buy out your contract, it's because they really want to have you on board and will offer a better rate to do so.

Aside from having you work for the client on a trial basis, a temp to hire situation helps HR departments minimize the costs and time associated with hiring and releasing workers.

Other methods of compensation

In the case of interim executives, there's a negotiated gross amount based on the estimated time to complete the assignment.

The payout is usually on a monthly or bi-weekly basis and in many cases, bonuses are negotiated for the completion of project deliverables. Travel and living expenses are included in the gross amount; however, other "extra" travel and living perks can be negotiated. For example, if an executive needs to travel out of state, she may negotiate an executive apartment, travel home on weekends, a living stipend, etc. The company should supply the necessary tools to complete the assignment such as a place to work, computer, software, cell phone, PDAs, wireless devices, office support, etc.

Hiring Bonuses, Post Project Delivery Bonuses, and Other Perks

In a tight labor market, many companies will offer perks to hire full-time workers with skills that are in strong demand. This practice holds true for agencies seeking to build their resource pool with highly desirable, top-level talent. Perks such as signing bonuses, referral bonuses, and paychecks between assignments are popular among specialty IT positions and high level executives.

Signing bonuses

The practice of signing bonuses has been used among movie producers and professional athletes for years. It's an incentive intended to motivate top talent to sign with a particular agency or company for a specified period of time and the practice is beginning to infiltrate the recruiting process. Signing bonuses are offered if you are a top producer in your field, you possess unique skills that are not easily found in the general labor supply, or the demand for your skills far exceeds the supply. Agencies looking to beef up their pool of top-level executives or other in-demand resources would offer a signing bonus to attract and keep talent.

In fact, a recent Recruiters Network white paper (*www.recruitersnetwork.com/whitepapers/bonuses.htm/*) suggests that hiring bonuses are becoming the rule rather than the exception in the IT profession. The paper suggests that the demand for qualified IT professionals has far out-paced the supply heating the competition for IT recruits.

Because of the high demand, agencies and consultancies have empowered IT professionals to set the terms of their employment. Consequently, many companies have resorted to aggressive bonus plans, both financial and other perks such as automobile leases, vacations, etc.

Post project delivery bonuses

Negotiated up front, post project delivery bonuses are usually reserved for executives and managers. For example, a finance executive that saves a company a substantial amount of money negotiates a percentage of the annual savings in the form of a post project bonus.

Availability retainer

Another perk provided by agencies to retain top-level executive talent is to offer regular weekly paychecks while on hiatus from a previous assignment. Many agencies retain you while marketing and selling your services. This can sometimes prevent you from taking on other projects. However, it provides a steady paycheck. Carefully define "availability" when negotiating your contract. You should be able to negotiate the ability to take on short-term projects during downtime between agency assignments.

Benefits

Many agencies and consultancies today offer healthcare benefits to their consultants. Eligibility requirements differ from plan to plan, but with the growing expense of healthcare coverage, this can be a valuable perk when considering an agency.

In addition to healthcare benefits, many companies also offer tax-deferred retirement plans such as 401K plans and other tax-deferred programs like dependent care reimbursement. Other perks include direct deposit, paid vacation (usually based on working a specific amount of consecutive hours), and specialized training programs in your field.

Compensation and the Independent Contractor

According to the U.S. Department of Labor Bureau of Labor Statistics, current Population Survey, "Contingent and Alternative Work Arrangements," there are over eight million independent contractors who comprise about 6 percent of the U.S. contingent workforce. The median weekly earning of full-time independent contractors is $640, according to a 1999 Bureau of Labor Statistics Current Population Survey Supplement on Contingent and Alternative Work Arrangements. Half of you will earn more than that number and half will earn less.

Contract work encompasses a wide variety of professions and the hourly rate varies depending on profession and the demand for those skills. The following list from George T. Silvestri's *Monthly Labor Review*, provides some of the occupations with the largest job growth for a 10-year period from1996 to 2006.

- ❖ Database administrators, computer support specialists, and all other computer scientists.
- ❖ Computer engineers.
- ❖ Systems analysts.
- ❖ Home health aides.
- ❖ Secondary school and special education teachers.
- ❖ Marketing and sales worker supervisors.
- ❖ Clerical supervisors and managers.
- ❖ Food service and lodging managers.
- ❖ Social workers.

It's no surprise that computer and IT related fields are in high demand. Within the IT profession, certain skills are in even greater demand such as programmers experienced in a particular programming language. Expect to command a higher hourly rate for specialty skills in which supply hasn't outpaced demand. According to a recruiting professional, other resources in demand include:

❖ Human resources trainers and educators.

❖ Recruiters.

❖ Engineers and re-engineers (business process engineering).

Estimated Hourly Rates for a Variety of Occupations

Note that the following rates are based on 1998 median ranges and are approximate 20 to 30 percent below today's actual rates. A list of salary comparison Web sites is at the end of the chapter.

Occupation	Range of hourly rates
Accountants and Auditors	$11.00 - $36.00+
Administrative Services Managers	$11.00 - $43.00+
Artists and Related Workers	$9.00 - $31.00+
Biological Scientists	$13.00 - $41.00+
Chemical Engineers	$20.00 - $44.00+
Chemists, Except Biochemists	$14.00 - $41.00+
Civil Engineers, Including Traffic	$16.00 - $42.00+
Claims Examiners, Property and Casualty Insurance	$11.00 - $38.00+
Clerical and Administrative Support Workers	$6.00 - $17.00+
Communications, Transportation, and Utilities Operations Managers	$13.00 - $44.00+
Computer Engineers	$18.00 - $45.00+
Computer Programmer Aides	$9.00 - $23.00+
Computer Programmers	$15.00 - $43.00+
Computer Support Specialists	$11.00 - $35.00+
Construction Managers	$13.00 - $43.00+
Credit Analysts	$11.00 - $35.00+
Database Administrators	$14.00 - $41.00+
Dental Hygienists	$12.00 - $39.00+
Dentists	$22.00 - $60.00+

Figure 4.2 (Source: Bureau of Labor Statistics median wage estimates for full-time employees, 1998)

Occupation	Range of hourly rates
Designers, Except Interior Designers	$7.00 - $33.00+
Dietitians and Nutritionists	$10.00 - $25.00+
Drafters	$10.00 - $26.00+
Economists, Including Market Research Analysts	$13.00 - $46.00+
Electrical and Electronic Engineering Technicians and Technologists	$10.00 - $30.00+
Electrical and Electronic Engineers	$18.00 - $44.00+
Employment Interviewers, Private or Public Employment Service	$9.00 - $35.00+
Financial Analysts, Statistical	$13.00 - $53.00+
Financial Managers	$13.00 - $57.00+
First-Line Supervisors and Managers/Supervisors - Clerical and Administrative Support Workers	$9.00 - $25.00+
First-Line Supervisors and Managers/Supervisors - Sales and Related Workers	$8.00 - $35.00+
Food Service and Lodging Managers	$7.00 - $22.00+
General Managers and Top Executives	$11.00 - $60.00+
Health Diagnosing and Treating Practitioners	$10.00 - $45.00+
Industrial Engineers, Except Safety	$17.00 - $42.00+
Industrial Production Managers	$15.00 - $47.00+
Lawyers	$18.00 - $60.00+
Legal Secretaries	$9.00 - $22.00+
Librarians, Professional	$11.00 - $33.00+
Management Analysts	$15.00 - $43.00+
Marketing, Advertising, and Public Relations Managers	$14.00 - $56.00+
Mathematical Scientists	$11.00 - $39.00+
Mechanical Engineers	$17.00 - $42.00+
Medical Scientists	$14.00 - $52.00+
Nuclear Engineers	$23.00 - $51.00+

Figure 4.2 (continued)

Occupation	Range of hourly rates
Occupational Therapists	$15.00 - $42.00+
Opticians, Dispensing and Measuring	$7.00 - $18.00+
Optometrists	$12.00 - $60.00+
Paralegal Personnel	$10.00 - $24.00+
Personnel, Training, and Labor Relations Managers	$12.00 - $44.00+
Personnel, Training, and Labor Relations Specialists	$10.00 - $36.00+
Pharmacists	$20.00 - $43.00+
Physical Therapists	$17.00 - $44.00+
Physician Assistants	$9.00 - $42.00+
Public Relations Specialists and Publicity Writers	$10.00 - $34.00+
Purchasing Managers	$11.00 - $42.00+
Radiologic Technologists	$11.00 - $23.00+
Registered Nurses	$14.00 - $33.00+
Sales Agents, Advertising	$8.00 - $40.00+
Sales Agents, Securities, Commodities, and Financial Services	$11.00 - $60.00+
Sales Agents, Selected Business Services	$8.00 - $38.00+
Sales Engineers	$15.00 - $47.00+
Sales Representatives, Scientific and Related Products and Services	$12.00 - $46.00+
Secretaries, Except Legal and Medical	$7.00 - $17.00+
Social Workers, Medical and Psychiatric	$10.00 - $24.00+
Speech-Language Pathologists and Audiologists	$13.00 - $39.00+
Statisticians	$14.00 - $42.00+
Stenographers and/or Court Reporters	$8.00 - $19.00+
Systems Analysts, Electronic Data Processing	$16.00 - $42.00+
Technical Writers and Editors	$12.00 - $38.00+

Figure 4.2 (continued)

While the previous chart is by no means a de facto standard, it provides a general guideline. Many consultants are earning more that the rates listed. These rates are fully loaded, which means they include benefits and other compensation, so most independent consultants will charge more than the listed rate to cover the cost of health and disability insurance. Other variables that affect the hourly rate include geographic area, experience level, and of course, supply and demand for your skills. Most of the salary related Web sites allow you to account for these variables in the sort criteria. To convert the annual salary and benefits package to a comparable hourly rate, simply divide the annual salary by 1000. You can try some of the following sites to compare rates:

- ❖ *www.dbm.com/jobguide/salary.html* (this is the Riley Guide mentioned earlier).

- ❖ *www.salary.com* (this site is a popular link on many business sites).

- ❖ *www.realrates.com* (site created by Janet Ruhl, author specializing in books on computer consulting).

- ❖ *www.careerjournal.com* (part of *The Wall Street Journal Online*).

Summary

Compensation is dependent on supply and demand for your services, as well as your skill level at performing those services. As it relates to monetary payments, compensation can take on several forms from hourly or daily rates to per project fees. There are other forms of monetary compensation such as bonuses and retainers that are often negotiated between agencies and consultants to attract and retain the best talent. Non-monetary compensation is another method of attracting and retaining talent by offering healthcare benefits, tax deferred programs, and other perks. Know your worth before negotiating. Visit salary sites on the Internet or check your local papers for similar jobs in your area. With an idea of your worth and the market for your skills, you'll have the necessary information to negotiate the best rate.

Key Points

❖ Remember, the amount of leverage you have depends on the skills you possess, your level of proficiency, the demand for those skills, and the size of the resource pool.

❖ Know the market rate for your skills before negotiating with potential clients or agencies.

❖ Carefully review agency policies to determine your eligibility for various benefits.

❖ Be wary of huge sign on bonuses or other perks that may come with non-compete or other restrictions. There's no substitute for sound legal advice. Have a lawyer review contracts before you sign them. The up-front legal fee can be a lot less than costly litigation later.

Action plan

At this point, you should have the resources you need to determine your market value and assess the competitive landscape. Take some time to formulate your compensation goals.

1. Visit a few salary sites and determine the going rate for your skills.

2. Calculate your hourly rate by dividing the full-time salary by 1,000.

3. Meet with at least one independent contractor to learn firsthand how to handle the topic of compensation and rate negotiation.

4. Determine your ideal rate and have an idea of the best alternative.

5. Identify other alternatives to your ideal rate that could provide added benefit, such as equity or partnerships.

6. If you're planning to work through an agency, what combination of benefits or added perks might entice you to sign with a particular agency?

7. Most importantly, can you afford to live on or remain profitable with the negotiated rate?

8. If the answer to number seven is no, then what alternative arrangements can be made? What expenses can you cut or reduce? Have you checked with more than one agency to compare rates? For how long can you work at that rate and build your experience portfolio or become eligible for agency paid training? Can additional training increase your rate? Would the agency be willing to train you?

9. Under what circumstances, if any, would you consider a temp to hire arrangement?

Agency Agreements and Employment Contracts

Whether you are working through an agency or independently, this section will help you understand important contractual considerations, especially when you want to make a change.

As a W2 of an agency, you'll most likely complete a single blanket agreement that will cover the assignments on which the agency places you for the duration of the agreement. Agreements exist between you and the agency. The agency completes an agreement with the client. You should sign an independent contractor agreement for each client you obtain even if you're working through an agency. This should be considered your letter of understanding of the assignment. It protects you from doing things that fall outside of your area of expertise. It defines what you'll be accountable for delivering and prevents the company from broadening the scope of what is expected. For example, highly paid help desk technicians without clearly defined agreements were asked to move and unpack boxes of computers during downtime. Without a clearly defined agreement, they had no recourse from the company that felt it was simply utilizing excess human capacity.

Agency Agreements

Agency agreements spell out your relationship as a temporary consultant to both the agency and client, the services that you'll provide, your rate, billing and payment schedules, eligibility for benefits, contract dates, extensions, and most likely, noncompete and nondisclosure clauses.

Agencies agree to provide your services to a given client for a specified period of time or the duration of a specific project. If you fail to stay on for that amount of time, then based upon the contractual agreement, you as the consultant may be liable for a financial nondelivery penalty if you do not exit per your termination clause. In other words, depending on the level and scope of your responsibilities, you are required to give the agency time to make alternative arrangements. For example, you accept an assignment and the contract stipulates that you must give 30 days' notice before exiting the assignment or you become liable for damages. If you fail to comply, then you would be liable for potential damages up to, but not to exceed, a certain dollar amount specified in the contract. If you fulfill your 30-day obligation, then you have no liability or further obligations. Usually, two to four weeks is standard for most positions. The agency has an obligation to keep the client satisfied, so it's not favorable for the agency to have recruits leave an assignment after a short period of time or before the project is complete. However, that's the risk an agent runs and it's their motivation to find the right match for each project.

The agency agreement helps reduce the agency's liability with the client. It ensures that you'll be available to work as needed to satisfy a particular client's project requirements. For example, an agency specializing in help desk personnel would have help desk consultants sign an agreement that they would be available to work when called. This is especially important in a help desk environment as many agencies are expected by their clients to provide resources "on-demand" to handle heavy volume peaks.

Additionally, most agencies will ask you to sign a noncompete clause to prevent you from going directly to agency clients as a 1099 or being directly hired by the client without a release. Agency noncompete clauses are purely of a financial concern to ensure that the agency is paid should you decide to seek employment with the same company, department, division, or manager either directly or through a third party. Such an agreement is usually in effect for a certain period of time that can range from six months or longer. Noncompete clauses that go beyond a year or are excessively restrictive should be suspect. For example, a noncompete that prevents you from seeking employment with the same company at any division or for any manager could substantially reduce your ability to gain employment, especially if the company from which you're restricted is a key player in your industry specialty. Avoid signing such excessively restrictive clauses at all costs.

It's important to clearly understand the terms of your agency agreement before signing it. If you're not certain or you have doubts about any clauses, particularly restrictive clauses, have a lawyer take a look at it. It only takes a lawyer about an hour and approximately $150 to $200 to review an agreement, which may be well worth it. There are also legal Web sites with forums that allow you to post questions to legal "experts." Visit the following for cursory legal assistance:

❖   *www.Counsel.net.*

❖   *www.Prairielaw.com.*

Can I pursue other contract work independent of the agency?

Unless you're paid a retainer to work specifically for the agency, most agencies won't preclude you from seeking your own contract work as long as it's not with agency clients. If the agency is paying you for downtime between assignments as a retainer to guarantee your availability, then you are prohibited from taking on other contract work. Make sure you negotiate the ability to take on small projects if the agency retainer doesn't pay what you could otherwise make on assignment or doesn't cover your expenses. Many permanent temps work with two or more agencies to ensure a steady flow of project work. Having backup agencies reduces potential downtime and lost income as a result of a poorly performing agency.

The downside of more than one agency is that you risk being unavailable when agency B calls if you're on assignment for agency A. Continued unavailability when called lessens your chances of remaining in the agency's priority pool. On the other hand, it helps you determine which agency finds more assignments. Another drawback of working with more than one agency is that it can take longer to accrue the required hours to obtain benefits. Some eligibility requirements for benefits depend on the accrual of a certain number of *consecutive* hours. Downtime between assignments may force the accrual process to begin again from zero hours. If benefits are important, you'll need to understand the agency's eligibility requirements before you sign.

Employment Contracts

Regularly used for full-time positions, employment contracts are becoming even more common in the world of permanent temping. Employment contracts are popular in the technical area and in executive level positions, and may also be used at the administrative level, depending on the sensitivity of information to which you'll be exposed.

As organizations outsource a growing amount of mission critical work, permanent temps are working at higher levels within organizations as well as with more sensitive information, making contracts the employers' defense against potential trade piracy and industrial espionage. Employment contracts also protect the permanent temp from bait and switch tactics. A bait and switch tactic entices you to work for a company with the promise of various compensatory benefits and perks. Then, after you begin working, they switch their original offer to something less desirable. As a permanent temp, an employment contract should be negotiated for a direct relationship (usually in the case of full-time employment), whereas an agency agreement should be negotiated for a subcontracted relationship (usually in an agency arrangement) and can be in addition to a subcontractor agreement.

Noncompete and nondisclosure agreements

Noncompete clauses in the context of an agency relationship are portions of employment contracts or letters of agreement that restrict you from working for the same company directly or indirectly through a third party without remuneration to the agency who first placed you there.

In the context of permanent employment situations, noncompete clauses restrict you from working for a competitor for a certain period of time. It would be rare for a company to ask an independent consultant to sign a noncompete agreement. A consultant working independent of an agency should not sign a noncompete clause. A noncompete to an independent consultant would be excessively restrictive and prevent you from gaining employment within your area of expertise. The nature of consulting is such that being an expert in your field; the likelihood of working for industry rivals is part and parcel of being an independent consultant.

Nondisclosure agreements are also known as confidentiality agreements. The purpose of the nondisclosure agreement is to prevent you from revealing, releasing, intimating, or in any way disclosing proprietary and confidential information during your employment, and for an indeterminate period of time thereafter, until such information becomes public via company release or otherwise after your employment. Failure to comply with a nondisclosure agreement subjects you to potentially severe penalties. This means that you can't discuss any information that the company deems confidential. Usually this involves information that, if divulged, could potentially put the company at an unfair competitive advantage.

This is an area where many consultants have gotten themselves in trouble from something as simple as discussing confidential information in casual conversation, to blatant divulgence. The company determines whether or not something outside of the public domain is confidential. Types of information that are considered confidential include:

- ❖ Product information on existing products or products in the development stage.

- ❖ Process information.

- ❖ Services information.

- ❖ Ideas—perhaps you were part of an initial brainstorming meeting where new ideas were imparted.

- ❖ Technology.

- ❖ Inventions.

- ❖ Patents.

- ❖ Contracts.

- ❖ Strategic business plans.

- ❖ Financial information that's not in the public domain.

- ❖ Customer lists.

- ❖ Prospect lists.

- ❖ Marketing plans.

- ❖ Trade secrets.

Information that is already in the public domain or the subsequent release of information to the public domain (through no fault of the contractor/consultant) is not considered confidential.

The following examples are typical of the type of language and the limitations set forth in noncompete clauses. As with any legally binding agreement, seek the advice of an attorney or legal professional before signing.

Sample noncompete and nondisclosure agreements

(Reproduced with permission from CCH Business Owner's Toolkit, published and copyrighted by CCH INCORPORATED, 2700 Lake cook Road, Riverwoods, IL, USA 60015, *www.toolkit.cch.com*.)

Example 1:

Nondisclosure and Noncompetition. (a) At all times while this agreement is in force and after its expiration or termination, [*employee name*] agrees to refrain from disclosing [*company name*]'s customer lists, trade secrets, or other confidential material. [*Employee name*] agrees to take reasonable security measures to prevent accidental disclosure and industrial espionage.

(b) While this agreement is in force, the employee agrees to use [*his/her*] best efforts to [*describe job*] and to abide by the nondisclosure and noncompetition terms of this agreement; the employer agrees to compensate the employee as follows: [*describe compensation*]. After expiration or termination of this agreement, [*employee name*] agrees not to compete with [*company name*] for a period of [*number*] years within a [*number*] mile radius of [*company name and location*]. This prohibition will not apply if this agreement is terminated because [*company*] violated the terms of this agreement.

Competition means owning or working for a business of the following type: [*specify type of business employee may not engage in*]

(c) [*Employee name*] agrees to pay liquidated damages in the amount of $[*dollar amount*] for any violation of the covenant not to compete contained in subparagraph (b) of this paragraph.

IN WITNESS WHEREOF, [*company name*] and [*employee name*] have signed this agreement.

_____

[company name]

_____

[employee's name]

Date: _____

Example 2:

This example is part of a larger agreement, such as an employment contract or an employee handbook. You can use it as a separate agreement or incorporate it into another, larger document.

Nondisclosure and Noncompetition. (a) After expiration or termination of this agreement, [*employee name*] agrees to respect the confidentiality of [*company name*] patents, trademarks, and trade secrets, and not to disclose them to anyone.

(b) [*Employee name*] agrees not to make use of research done in the course of work done for [*company name*] while employed by a competitor of [*company name*].

(c) [*Employee name*] agrees not to set up in business as a direct competitor of [*company name*] within a radius of [*number*] miles of [*company name and location*] for a period of [*number and measure of time* (e.g., "four months" or "10 years")] following the expiration or termination of this agreement.

(d) [*Employee name*] agrees to pay liquidated damages of $[*dollar amount*] if any violation of this paragraph is proved or admitted.

IN WITNESS WHEREOF, [*company name*] and [*employee name*] have signed this agreement.

_____

[company name]

_____

[employee name]

Date: _____

Sample independent contractor agreement

See Appendix B for a comprehensive agreement.

Sample limit of liability contract clause

The example below is common language found in an independent contractor or agency agreement concerning the contractor's professional liability. Professional liability is the contractor's exposure to risk if his or her work causes a problem. For example, your software code resulted in an error that crashed operators' systems. Setting a limit of liability reduces your or your agency's payout should the company decide to sue for consequential damages.

Example:

> [*Independent contractor name*] is not an employee of the company. It is agreed that [*Independent contractor name*] maximum liability hereunder for any determined negligence or misconduct shall not exceed [*Independent contractor name*] fees billed during the three (3) month period with respect to his activity, and in no event shall he be liable for any consequential damages or special damages. Please confirm your acknowledgement and acceptance of these terms by signing this agreement where indicated below.

Negotiating your contract

You don't have to sign a contract that you're uncomfortable with. It's always best to try and negotiate a contract with which you're more comfortable. Be patient, this could take a few rounds of negotiation. Be suspect of agencies or clients who pressure you to sign a contract immediately. Consult a legal professional for advice on contracts that you suspect are questionable.

Not all positions warrant the leverage to negotiate. That, of course, depends on the supply and demand for your skills as well as the type of position sought. Remember that agreements don't have to be "take it or leave it" propositions. If you have a better alternative, it's worth bringing it to the table.

What's negotiable? Depending on your level and the supply and demand for your expertise, almost everything can be negotiable. Typical elements of negotiation include:

❖ Special bonuses such as signing bonuses, early completion bonuses, bonuses as a percentage of savings realized as a result of your work.

❖ Holiday and or sick pay (usually agency related).

❖ Amount of accrued hours before becoming eligible for benefits (usually agency related).

❖ Working hours (for example, 8 a.m. to 4 p.m. as opposed to 9:00 to 5:00).

❖ Paid training for skills upkeep and maintenance (usually agency related).

❖ Fees and subscriptions to relevant industry associations, journals, and Web sites (usually agency related; however, can be required by the client. For example, you're a consulting physician who's been asked by the company to attend an industry conference. The company should pay any associated fees along with your travel and living expenses for the duration of the conference.)

❖ Health club memberships.

❖ Reimbursement for travel or other travel related or commuting expenses (carefully define and negotiate travel-related expenses such as tolls and public transportation costs).

❖ Adjusted rates and/or time on a sliding scale as the project nears completion. (For example, a project may take more up front time in the form of research or other activities. You might negotiate for a higher rate for the extensive research up front, then adjust it down as the project progresses.)

Remember that the amount of leverage you possess depends on the supply and demand for your skills as well as your industry reputation. While this is not to suggest that any of the above mentioned items can be negotiated, you should at least be prepared to make an offer if you believe that it makes working with a particular client or agency more acceptable. Use the previous list for ideas to help you obtain a better or more palatable arrangement.

What's not negotiable? Usually ownership of any property, physical or intellectual, during your contract with a given organization is not negotiable. Types of property include patents, technologies, inventions, copyrights, specifications, designs, software code, etc. You may, however, with permission, use some of the aforementioned items to help you obtain additional contracts. For example, a Web site designer or information architect could obtain permission to use copyrighted designs and navigational schemes in his portfolio.

At certain levels and for certain types of positions where the supply is adequate, there may be little room for monetary negotiation. In these cases, time and flexibility can become effective elements in gaining a more palatable arrangement. For example, a help desk technician who may be at the limits of the hourly rate could possibly negotiate working different hours, so that he could attend a class during off hours. Better yet, the technician may be able to negotiate the training as a means to improve his or her skill level to earn a higher hourly rate.

Another alternative to monetary negotiation is to accept a lesser rate but extend the duration of the contract. This will enable you to pick up additional contract work to supplement your existing contract without negatively impacting the project's deliverables time frame.

Changing Jobs

Eventually it happens... you've been with a company and you're ready to move on. It can result from project completion, boredom, or overall dissatisfaction. For executives, it may be a little tougher to simply change depending on contractual arrangements. At the implementer and some analyst job functions, it's as simple as contacting your agency or broker to discuss your next move. That's the advantage of temping. There are, however, some considerations to make.

Carefully review your employment contract to understand the legal implications of leaving an assignment before completion. If it's a case where the assignment has undergone a major change or the assignment was completed prior to the time frame, discuss the situation with your broker or agency representative. It's rarely a good idea to leave an assignment before completion; however, under some circumstances it may be warranted. Check with your agency representative, broker, or legal professional to determine your contractual obligations if the client goes bankrupt or merges with or is acquired by another company, which may change the scope or definition of your existing project.

In many implementer or knowledge-based functional positions (refer to the chart in Chapter 1) there is more flexibility to change jobs without legal ramifications. However, there may be agency issues if your stay is so brief that the company barely recoups its training investment. For example, if you're working as a help desk technician for an agency client and you want to change because you prefer a different office culture or environment, most likely your agency will be able to find a more suitable organization for you without too much effort. On the other hand, if you are looking to make a change every three or four months, then it costs the agency more in terms of marketing dollars and goodwill with clients to continually search for new assignments on your behalf. At this point, it becomes detrimental to your agency relationship and perhaps your agency agreement to change assignments frequently.

If you're not under contract for a specified period of time, and you want to remain in favor with your agency, stay the minimum amount of time necessary before deciding to change.

Changing agencies

It's in the agency's best interest to find a job that satisfies your professional interests, because when you're satisfied, you're more productive and that bodes well for the agency's client, too. Occasionally, you'll find that you can't seem to establish a good rapport with your agency and for your own personal well-being, the satisfaction of the client, and the reputation of the agency, it becomes necessary to switch to a different agency.

Make certain that you're not liable for any fees if you decide to sign with another agency. Carefully review any noncompete or other restrictive clauses that may be included in your agency agreement. Taking on assignments with agency clients, even if they approach you knowing that you no longer work for the agency, could be a breach of a noncompete or restrictive agreement. Under these circumstances you and/or the client of your former agency could be liable for various contract buyout fees or commissions.

Summary

Agency agreements, employment contracts, and nondisclosure and noncompete clauses are all part of today's work culture. Designed to protect you and your agency, they shouldn't be excessively restrictive in any way. As a permanent temp, you'll want to negotiate a fair contract that allows you the freedom and flexibility to make changes. Remember that the time to question an agreement is *before* signing it.

Key points:

❖ Thoroughly understand the terms of your agency agreement *before* you sign it. If benefits are an important reason for signing with an agency, understand exactly how to become eligible for benefits or other agency perks.

❖ Employment contracts and independent contractor agreements should also be thoroughly understood before signing. Better yet, have your lawyer or legal professional review the contract to make certain there are no excessively restrictive clauses.

❖ Don't allow yourself to be pressured to sign any agreement with which you are not comfortable—especially if it seems as though you must sign immediately. Be suspect of any agreements that require immediate signatures and consult the advice of a legal professional to make certain the contract is reasonable.

❖ Changing jobs is easier at certain job functions and job levels. Understand the extent of your contractual obligations to either the client or agency before pursuing a job change. Take notice of any noncompete and nondisclosure or confidentiality clauses that may be in effect.

Action Plan

In the previous chapter, we discussed compensation and rates. This chapter is where you'll negotiate a formal agreement or contract based on your desired compensation along with other perks and stipulations.

1. Assess the amount of leverage you may have during negotiation based on your functional level within the organization and the supply and demand for your skills.

2. Determine any monetary benefits that you might be able to negotiate such as signing bonuses or retainers.

3. Determine the non-monetary forms of benefits or perks that you might be able to negotiate in addition to or in lieu of items listed in number two. (i.e. benefits, training, flexible hours, equity stake, laptop computer, additional phone/fax lines installed in your home, other tools of the trade, etc.)

4. Based on your previous research of agencies and the market rate for your skills, weigh the various agreements to determine the best possible arrangement.

Marketing Yourself

Whether you choose to sign with an agency or become an independent contractor, you will need to consistently promote yourself and market your skills. This chapter will help you define your market, identify effective ways to target your market, and remain marketable in today's highly competitive career landscape.

Defining your market

Take a look at your profession. Do your services address the general market or do you specialize in a particular niche within the profession? Is your focus geographic, industry, or platform specific?

For example, a finance specialist might seek an interim management position within a variety of different companies across several industries. The market is broad in the sense that all companies require some type of financial manager. Depending on the individual's level of experience and the size of the company, the position can be a VP of finance, controller, or a director of corporate tax. The market is heavily dependent on the type of skill you possess as opposed to the industry or geographic location.

On the other hand, a computer consultant specializing in programming in a UNIX environment would focus on the types of companies running UNIX systems. Again, it's not industry dependent; however, the business size may be the best parameter such as mid to large businesses with high traffic networks are more conducive to the UNIX platform. Your skill niche, which in this case is programming in a UNIX environment, would define the market. A secondary parameter defining your market in this case might also include company size.

A marketing executive with extensive knowledge of and experience within the telecommunications industry would be an example of a market defined by industry. If this individual also had specific experience with the telecommunications industry in Europe, then there could also be a secondary geographic market.

When defining your market, look for common threads in the following areas to determine the most effective way to target your market:

- ❖ Geography: global, regional, country specific.

- ❖ Industry: broad scope, specific segment, old economy, new economy, emerging markets.

- ❖ Skill specialty: general executive leadership, managerial, professional, paraprofessional.

Identifying the Most Effective Ways to Target Your Market

Having defined your market, the task of targeting your market becomes easier. If your market is based on geographic parameters, a good way to reach your market is through targeted direct mail (postal or electronic). Locate the companies within your region through local business directories, industry associations, or through Web sites focused on a specific geographic area. Some geographic areas publish their own periodicals from which you may be able to rent their subscriber list.

To reach a more mass audience, if the concentration of potential clients is within a specific location, you may also run a small space ad in the online and/or offline versions of the local paper's classified section.

For example, if you want to utilize your dotcom start-up knowledge, you would begin your search by seeking new media companies located in the Silicon Valley, Silicon Alley, and the Boston 128 Corridor locations. You could then plan a strategy based on the following tactics:

❖ Look for online or offline publications in which to run a small classified ad.

❖ Seek Web sites that have geographic specific searches, such as Yahoo, and post your resume or a small classified ad.

❖ Link your Web site to the sites where your classified ads or resume postings are located.

❖ Join a bulletin board site whose members may have use for your services. **A word of caution here:** bulletin boards are give and take propositions and generally members who blatantly promote their services are "flamed" (admonished by other members). If you plan on using this approach, then plan on becoming an active participating member. This method will take time to build credibility and earn the respect of fellow peers. It's usually acceptable to create a *brief* signature that tells what you do. A signature is your sign-on I.D. such as your name and can include additional text, for example: *CIOPro—Executive consulting for information systems development.* Do not rely on bulletin boards as a primary networking tool because they can become time intensive. Also, when posting a question or response, be wary of leaving detailed information, such as client information, as some participants are not straightforward.

❖ Offer to teach a course in your field at a local college or university.

❖ Become active in your alumni association through alumni newsletter articles and updates on your professional milestones.

❖ Write an article and have it published it in a trade journal, periodical, or on a Web site. Target the specific places where your prospects go. If you're unable to publish it in a journal or periodical, then publish it on your own Web site.

❖ Look for relevant trade shows (online and offline), rent the list of attendees and conduct a direct mail campaign.

Similarly, the marketing executive mentioned in an earlier example with experience in the European telecommunications industry would seek opportunities with European companies or other companies seeking to do business in Europe. The strategy in this case would encompass both industry and geographic parameters. The tactics may include:

❖ Obtain the mail lists of trade associations with executive memberships in Europe or multinational telecom companies that conduct business in Europe.

❖ Run a classified in a general executive level trade journal or executive marketing journal or Web site. If the majority of these multinationals have offices in a particular city, target a major local paper or periodical that executives would read, such as *Crain's New York Business*.

❖ Participate in trade associations that are either industry or profession related.

❖ Participate in newsgroups pertinent to the telecommunications industry. You should first determine if the type of person that would make decisions on temporary executives would visit bulletin boards or newsgroups.

❖ Offer to speak at a related seminar or industry association meeting. Many trade associations are always on the lookout for knowledgeable speakers.

It's faster and easier to start with your immediate network of school alumni and industry organizations to build credibility and establish yourself in a space where you may already be known. Regardless of your industry or profession, self-promotion is essential to building awareness, gaining recognition, and obtaining clients.

Never Underestimate the Power of Networking

Networking is the art of turning your contacts into business opportunities either directly or indirectly. Networking involves identifying your warm market and staying in touch with them to expand your sphere of influence and obtain new business opportunities.

Self-promotion is uncomfortable for many independent professionals, but with preparation and practice, it becomes easier. It's really a mindset that you'll eventually adopt that helps uncover opportunities that might not have otherwise surfaced.

What's my "warm market"?

Your warm market consists of friends, colleagues, business associates, etc. that you remain in contact with on a fairly regular basis. Dust off your PDAs, Palms, and Daytimers. Think of all the people you've been in contact with over the past 12 to18 months and compile a list. The list should include members of industry associations, college alumni associations, current or former supervisors, managers, and co-workers. Other areas to consider outside of business relationships are local clubs; health clubs; sporting colleagues such as racquetball partners, golfing partners, etc.; neighbors; religious affiliations; parents clubs or children's organizations such as soccer teams, little league, dance, and other sporting or creative associations.

You'll be surprised at how many different contacts you come up with when you take the time to go through your contact lists. Don't second-guess which contacts may be in a position to help you. Include all likely prospects and if you're not sure, include them anyway. Part of the exercise is to build awareness and even if they can't help you today, they might be able to refer you to someone who can or keep you on file when an opportunity arises.

The next step in networking is to contact these people with an update on what you're doing and a genuine interest in what they're doing also. You'll need to develop your 30-second "elevator pitch" that concisely explains exactly what you're your doing and what you need. For example, let's say you're a banking consultant and you strike up a conversation with a managerial or executive type in an elevator. While en route to your floor, the person asks, "What do you do?" You're reply should sound something like this, "I'm an executive from a middle tier bank with 25 years' international funds transfer experience. I'm looking for the opportunity to consult with banks interested in getting involved in this area. I need to speak to people in currency and arbitrage trading. What's the best way to reach these people?" *Ding...* you reach your floor, exchange cards, and add another member to your network.

Remember, networking, similar to Internet discussion groups and bulletin boards, is a give and take activity. The contacts from your warm market become part of your "house list" and should be updated regularly. Maintaining an accurate house list is an important part of preventing your warm market from turning cold.

If your warm market is too large to phone each contact, consider a direct mail program. Create a brief letter describing your services that asks readers to pass along your name to colleagues who could use your services. Around the holidays is a good time to rekindle relationships. Remember to include several business cards along with a self-addressed, stamped business reply card. Your personal deliverables statement, created in Chapter 3, and the benefits of what you're offering will come in handy here. Your business reply card should include simple check boxes with at least the following information:

☐ Yes, call me. We could use your help on a project now.

☐ I don't have a need right now. Try again on [*month/ date*].

☐ Remove me from your mail list.

Add a separate section for the prospect's name, address, phone, e-mail, etc.

Where should I network?

Networking can take place virtually anywhere. Always keep an ample supply of business cards with you and your finger on the trigger, ready to dole out cards instinctively as you meet new people and potential clients. Networking can sometimes occur casually during a commute on the train or bus or while waiting in an airport. Your personal deliverables statement should appear somewhere on your business card so that what you do is clear when a prospect pulls out your card several weeks or even months later. **A word of caution:** keep your card clear and legible. If placing your deliverables statement crowds your card, then place it on the reverse side or condense it to less words. For example, "mergers and acquisitions business consulting" instead of "experienced in fast-track mergers and acquisitions for high-tech, fortune 500 companies."

More formal networking should include a visit to a networking event such as a seminar, industry association meeting, or trade show. Before attending an event, call the event sponsor and find out the demographics of attendees by title so that you're not wasting your time. Plan on joining at least one industry association and you'll quickly become added to the mail lists of several organizations sponsoring networking breakfasts, golf outings, seminars, etc. **A word of caution:** you could easily become a perpetual meeting attendee. Choose your networking events based on the relevance of the subject matter, type of people the meeting targets, and the potential for meeting qualified prospects. Look for networking events whose attendees are either users of your services or have influence in the decision to purchase your services.

Carefully budget your time so that you can attend networking events that yield the best potential clients. For example, an optical engineering consultant might consider attending a local or national optical society meeting. Although the attendees may be other optical engineers and not necessarily candidates for the engineer's services, they could be influential in their company's decision to hire an optical engineering consultant. The same optical engineer might also attend a seminar or event attended by companies that manufacture imaging products such as cameras, scanners, optical disk storage equipment, etc.

With many companies turning to the Web for seminars and meetings, the potential for online networking increases. Look into the possibility of becoming a guest speaker at a trade association "Webinar." Perhaps you could rent the addresses of participating attendees.

There are formal networking groups in which you pay an annual fee to network into new jobs and assignments. The principle behind professional networking groups is to bring people together for the exchange of ideas and business leads. Most meet regularly over breakfast or lunch and admission to the group is through a formal vote allowing one member per profession. For example, they wouldn't allow two copywriters in the same chapter unless their writing addressed completely different markets. Some of the larger networking groups are:

❖ LeTips (*www.letips.com*).

❖ Business Network International (*www.bni.com*).

❖ Ali Lassen's Lead Clubs (*www.leadsclub.com*).

Networking is really a frame of mind that comes with practice. Look for ways to turn current opportunities into networking events. For example, learn if a current client has ties to colleagues in the industry that might be in need of your services by planning a casual lunch with a co-worker or department manager. Perhaps the company has other divisions or affiliates on another floor or across town. Keep it casual and try not to spend too much working time on networking. Good times for off-hour networking opportunities can be during lunch or breaks, early in the morning before the workday begins, or after hours.

Creating the Ultimate Sales Presentation

The ultimate sales presentation should be concise, comprehensive, relevant to the audience, and must leave a lasting positive impression. A concise presentation gets right to the point while anticipating and answering questions the prospect may have. In order to do this, you need to research and understand the company so that you can tailor your presentation to the specific needs of the company.

For example, if you're a software programmer meeting with a company that develops banking software for transaction processing, begin by researching the company. Visit their Web site to learn about the company—their philosophy, recent news about the company, and if public, have an idea of their stock price. If possible, have an idea of the technology that they're using and the platform on which they're running. You might also visit Hoover's Online (*www.hooversonline.com*) to learn what other companies compete in the same market. Then, look for any similarities between your background and the company's background. Perhaps you've worked for one of their competitors or attended a recent conference on online banking.

Once you've gathered the data, begin creating the framework for your presentation, keeping in mind the three key criteria: 1) concise; 2) comprehensive; 3) relevant to the audience. Create a separate private area for miscellaneous ice-breaker type information and general information from which you may draw during the context of the presentation. For example, during the course of the presentation, the company representative asks what trends you are encountering in the online banking industry. This would be a good place to mention the recent online banking conference you had attended. You could also include the company's financial information here or any recent merger or acquisition activity.

Creating the ultimate sales presentation involves flexibility to target your specific market niches. Once your framework is developed, make it modular so that you can substitute information for fast, easy customization.

Typical modules should include the following:

1. Personal deliverables statement. This can be modified slightly if it better addresses the needs of the audience.

2. Describe other clients with whom you worked. Modify this area to list clients that are similar to your prospect. If you haven't worked with a great deal of clients, then rely on your experience and draw similarities between your experience and the job requirements.

3. Articulate your accomplishments with the other clients. You can modify this area to include accomplishments that are relevant to the prospect's situation.

4. Describe how you can accomplish successful results for your current prospect. To complete this module, you'll need to have qualified the prospect to understand their current situation, identify where they would like to be, and determine what constitutes a successful result.

5. Distribute any information that summarizes your presentation such as your resume, a brochure, or samples.

6. Never give your solution in your proposal. This is a pitfall of many novice consultants when asked to provide a solution to a prospect's problem. The idea is for the prospect to hire you first, then obtain your solution.

If the position involves working on a team, then demonstrate your team skills not only as a participant, but also in the other roles that emerge while working within the team context, such as facilitator, leader, or non-participant observer. If the position is for a leadership role, then demonstrate your leadership ability. For positions that involve major changes, you should show your ability to act as a catalyst.

The ultimate sales presentation not only articulates your competence at the tactical level, but also exudes a sense of confidence and a positive attitude that make you someone with whom others would benefit from working. Your skill is nearly as important as your ability to fit in with the organization. In other words, it doesn't matter how brilliant you are if you're impossible to work with.

Not all interviews or prospect visits require a formal PowerPoint slide presentation, but it's good to prepare a sample presentation using the modules previously discussed. Even if it's not necessary, you'll at least benefit from the thought process that goes into creating the presentation. Practice your presentation in front of a mirror, so that it becomes second nature to you. Role-play and put yourself in the audiences' shoes and ask and answer the questions that they would ask. The more comfortable you become with your presentation, the more natural it will come across to your prospects.

Keeping Yourself Marketable

Stephen Covey, in his highly acclaimed book and tape series, *The Seven Habits of Highly Effective People*, refers to this as habit number seven, "Sharpening the Saw." Tom Peters, author of *Innovation Revolution* and a number of other books and tapes on contemporary business, refers to it as "the brand called you." Yes, you're now a commodity, and in order to retain a high return, you must continue to invest in *you*.

While the company in which you're placed provides company orientation or training on the specific application area in which you were hired, you should also consider additional training such as specialized courses, advanced degrees, complementary degrees, or certification programs. Credentials can become one's key differentiator and oftentimes the deciding factor in getting the assignment.

For example, a marketing executive may wish to augment her expertise by obtaining certification in electronic commerce. Other examples in the technical field may include network, hardware, and software certifications. Check with industry vendors for ongoing education and certifications offered. One IS manager reports that he looks for people that not only have the IS background, but also additional certifications on the types of hardware and software specific to the job. So that if two candidates of similar backgrounds and experience were presented to work on his network of Cisco routers and one candidate possessed a Cisco certification, he would prefer the candidate with the Cisco certification.

The speed at which information and technology changes makes it essential to continue re-training in your specific discipline to either learn new skills or refresh existing skills. Revisiting our job function chart from Chapter 1, consider the following suggestions for keeping yourself marketable:

Executive/managerial

Because strategic vision and mission critical decision-making are significant functions within this role, consider education and training that pertains to overall changes in business environments that affect strategic decision-making. For example, e-commerce and electronic buying hubs have created a substantial impact on the way business is conducted. Savvy executives learn the strategic benefits of these channels to better prepare themselves for making effective business decisions on deployment of such technologies.

How can you remain current? As an alumnus of a particular business school, you'll most likely receive information on executive level retreats and seminars on emerging technologies and new business models for a new economy. Check the Web sites of graduate business schools such as University of Virginia's Darden Graduate Business School (*exed.darden.virginia.edu/index.htm*), Harvard Business School (*exed.hbs.edu/index.html*), University of Pennsylvania's Wharton Business School (*aresty-direct.wharton.upenn.edu/execed/index.cfm*), Stanford School of Business (*gsb.stanford.edu/exed*), Northwestern University's Kellogg Graduate of Management (*ExecEd@kellogg.nwu.edu*), and NYU's Stern School of Business (*stern.nyu.edu/execprgms*) for continuing executive education.

Other alternatives for continuing education include executive journals, magazines, and newspapers such as *Harvard Business Review*, *Fast Company Magazine*, *Business 2.0, Red Herring, Inc.*, and *The Wall Street Journal.*

Knowledge-based specialists (professional/technical/ managerial)

Because your job function depends heavily on your skills in a particular area, remaining marketable means staying current in your specific discipline. Continuing education through the college or university from which you graduated is a good starting point. You may wish to consider seminars and conferences offered through industry associations such as CPA Associates International for accounting professionals (*www.cpaai.com*). Associations also provide news and updates on important legislation affecting your discipline, new techniques, or other environmental factors that may impact your field, such as e-commerce and taxation. Other business oriented organizations offer courses in a wide variety of disciplines such as the American Management Association (*www.amanet.org*) and the Business Marketing Association (*www.marketing.org*).

If you haven't already done so, consider an advanced degree in your field such as an MBA or other graduate degree programs. Many advanced degrees are now offered as a distance learning program so you can attend class from your computer via the Internet. Type "distance learning" into a search engine and you'll find hundreds of degree and non-degree programs from colleges and universities throughout the world. Another distance learning site that compiles several sites by discipline is Distance Learning on the Net by Glenn Hoyle (*www.hoyle.com*).

You should also consider additional certification programs such as a CPA (certified public account), APICS (Educational Society for Resource Management, formerly the American Production and Inventory Control Society) specializing in manufacturing and resource planning certifications (*www.apics.org/*

Certification), or Help Desk Institute (*www.helpdeskinst.com/hdi-certification*) certifications for help desk and technical support professionals. Visit the Web site of your profession's trade association and look for the "certifications" section.

Implementers (administrators, technicians, programmers, paraprofessionals)

Similar to the knowledge-based specialist, your skill specialty requires periodic updating to ensure your marketability. Check with colleges and universities for continuing education programs. Many offer distance learning programs for credit and non-credit courses. Additional non-credit programs are available through industry and trade associations such as NCRA (National Court Reporters Association, *www.ncraonline.org/learn*), which also offers online seminars and certifications.

The hardware or software platform on which you specialize most likely offers a certification program such as Microsoft (*www.microsoft.com/trainingandservices*), Novell (*www.novell.com/education*), Oracle (*www.education.oracle.com*), Cisco (*www.cisco.com/warp/public/10/wwtraining*), Sun Microsystems (*www.suned.sun.com/HQ/certification*), and IBM (*www.ibm.com/services/learning*).

For specific software application training such as Word, WordPerfect, Project, etc., consider local or online training courses offered by independent computer training specialists such as New Horizons Computer Learning Centers (*www.newhorizons.com*), ExecuTrain (*www.exec:utrain.com*), and OneOnOne Computer Training (www.oootraining.com).

Adding to your experience portfolio is an ongoing and important part of keeping yourself marketable. Formal education and training can be obtained during downtime between assignments. If you're working through an agency, find out if they have a continuing education program or other training programs for skill maintenance and update.

Summary

Marketing yourself is an ongoing program of generating leads and qualified prospects. A good marketing program relies on a strategy for integrating all marketing vehicles such as advertising, direct mail, networking, etc. to gain the maximum yield of leads and new business opportunities. Keeping yourself marketable is tantamount to your marketing program. Continuing education and skills updates help ensure your marketability. Remember to continue marketing yourself even when business is good. A steady stream of leads will help ensure a more regular income with fewer downtime gaps.

Key points:

❖ It's important to define your market to make targeting easier and more cost-effective.

❖ Create an integrated program with which to target your market. Combine small space ads, postal and electronic direct mail, and online and offline networking to obtain valuable new prospects.

❖ Your marketing program must be ongoing. Don't stop marketing because you're on assignment. You need to constantly look for the next opportunity.

❖ Networking is an important part of marketing yourself. Remain in touch with your warm market and join at least one industry association to expand your networking efforts.

❖ Be prepared for networking opportunities by keeping a supply of business cards handy. Remember, many opportunities arise from casual situations such as a morning commute.

❖ Your sales presentation should be concise, comprehensive, and relevant to the audience. Use a modular approach in developing your presentation to allow for customization for specific prospects. Rehearse your presentation so that it sounds natural.

❖ Continue investing in *you*. Whether through formal classes, industry conferences or Webinars, training and skills updates are an important factor in keeping yourself marketable.

Action plan

At this point, you're ready to assemble your marketing plan.

1. Define your market based on the parameters mentioned earlier.

2. Examine the available marketing vehicles to determine the most effective way to target and reach your market.

3. Set aside one day to scour your contact list and create your "house list" of warm prospects.

4. Determine a reasonable timeframe in which to contact your warm market. (If you haven't decided whether the permanent temping lifestyle is for you, then base your date on a given amount of time after deciding to pursue permanent temping. In any case, it's still a smart career move to keep your warm contacts current.)

5. Join your local industry association chapter and plan to attend at least one networking event in the next one to two months. Obtain at least two or three qualified contacts at the networking event.

6. Create your ultimate sales presentation by starting with the modular outline described earlier.

7. Sign up for at least one free training program or seminar every three to four months or at least read a book in your field over the next six months. To maintain industry and technical expertise, it may be necessary for you to sign up for at least one paid course.

8. Attend industry conventions and network meetings.

Working As a Free Agent

Working as a free agent requires flexibility, persistence, a good sense of humor, and above all, impeccable organization skills including time management. This chapter will provide guidance on organizing yourself to become more effective as a permanent temp. It will also show you how to optimize client relationships to ensure repeat business.

Setting Up Your Office

You should have a specific office space where you will "go to work" each day. To control costs, consider a designated space within your home or apartment and if feasible, consider leasing space in a shared office or even an existing office as an alternative to renting office space outright. Shared offices are usually wired for Internet access and have a copier, fax, and other office equipment available. Some even provide administrative assistance.

If you decide on a home office, your office should be a comfortable room within your home or apartment where you have plenty of space for files, computer equipment, disk storage, reference books, and other miscellaneous office supplies. If you're planning to deduct a portion of your rent or mortgage for a home office, keep in mind the area must be exclusive, for regular office use and specifically for your trade or business. Chapter 8 discusses the regulations based on IRS Publication 587, *Business Use of Your Home*.

If you expect to do the majority of your work from your office, then it makes sense to have a complete desk setup for your home office. Invest in a comfortable chair with good back support and a desk that give you enough room for your computer, peripherals and a work area—milk crates and a bean bag chair don't count. If you're trying to squeeze an office into an already tight space, look into an office armoire. Basically, it's an office in a cabinet with shelves, drawers, a pullout keyboard tray, and usually a foldout "L" shaped workspace. They come in a variety of sizes and take up less room than a traditional desk setup. Plus, everything closes up easily for a neat, uncluttered appearance.

Keep a supply of business forms handy such as invoices (include your social security number or EIN, employer identification number, for tax purposes), letterhead, envelopes, and fax cover sheets. Most word processing software applications have preformatted templates that you can use for each of these forms. It's usually quite easy to customize them to your specific requirements such as adding a logo. With a majority of today's business being conducted online and via e-mail, you can print on-demand and save the expense of printing bulk quantities of each form.

Telecommunication equipment

Keep the lines of communication open for your clients. There's nothing worse than getting a busy signal or no answer when you call a business. A separate phone line for your business phone, fax machines, Internet, and personal phone is important. (As with office space, check with your accountant regarding write-off of the business phone line.) Otherwise, your clients may not be able to get through to you while you're on the other line or the Internet. At least have a separate phone and fax line. This way you'll be able to use your fax line to access the Internet without tying up your phone line. Another option is to consider a modem with a call-waiting feature or, if available in your area, cable or DSL modems that allow you to use your phone while on the Internet. There are numerous software packages that will allow you to fax directly from your computer. Another option is to use a modem that supports telephony and call from your computer using a microphone or headset. The sound quality can be lacking, but as improvements continue, the quality should improve by the time you read this.

It's more professional to have a separate business phone line; however, if you're trying to contain your initial startup costs, you might want to at least consider a telephone with two or three mailboxes that you can setup for personal and for business calls. Consider phone features that offer convenience such as a cordless phone, speakerphone, or headset. **A word of caution here:** make certain the phone equipment and service providers offer good, audible sound quality, especially if you plan to use Internet telephony. It is extremely frustrating to try to conduct business over inaudible phone lines or poor quality phone equipment. There's a limit on how cheap you can go without comprising quality.

Cellular phones are useful if you'll be spending a lot of time on the road or away from your office. Depending on the plan you choose, many cellular packages are quite cost-effective. If your line of work requires you to be immediately accessible, then consider optional services available through your cellular provider such as call forwarding from your landline to your cellular phone and voice mail. Some of these additional services come pre-packaged.

Do you really need to invest in a fax machine? Although you can send and receive faxes directly from your computer, oftentimes hard copy documents need to be faxed, such as signed contracts. It's time-consuming to interrupt your day to go to the local copy center. However, if you feel that in your line of work, faxing will be minimal, then try going without a fax machine initially or invest in an inexpensive or previously owned fax machine. You can always add a fax machine later, or better yet, buy a multipurpose fax/scanner/laser printer as a compromise.

Computer equipment

If you don't already own a computer system, now is the time to invest in one. There is a vast array of computer configurations available. Consider the type of work you'll be doing, the programs you'll be running, and how you plan to work (remote versus in your office) to determine the computing power and configuration you'll need. Talk to several local computer retailers to learn what's available in your budget. When it comes to computers, it pays to shop around. Ask other consultants in a similar field for their advice on purchasing the right computer for your needs. There are also hundreds of computing newsgroups that are usually very helpful and candid about what you should look for when selecting a computer.

If you plan to work outside of your home office the majority of the time and if you'll need mobility, consider a laptop/docking station computer setup. You buy a laptop, regular monitor, and a docking station. All your peripherals (standard size keyboard, monitor, printer, backup storage device, scanner, etc.) plug into the docking station, so that when you disconnect your computer, you simply remove it from the docking station without the hassles of unplugging all the peripherals. It's like having a desktop system, except you basically bring your hard drive with you. This setup gives you the mobility of a laptop with the larger keyboard and display options of a desktop.

Internet connectivity

If you don't already have an Internet Service Provider (ISP), you'll need to obtain one. Shop around for the best prices and if you don't mind a lot of advertising messages, the free mail services offer a cost-effective alternative. If, however, you're planning to conduct the majority of your business via the Internet, you'll need a reliable carrier that offers the server space requirements you'll need, especially if you plan to send and receive large files. Also use the fastest, affordable technology if you plan to use the Internet as the main business pipeline to your clients. The monthly cost to have a cable modem and ISP (usually included with the modem) is nearly the same as a separate phone line plus monthly ISP fee. DSL is slightly higher than a separate phone line and ISP combination.

Likewise, if you plan to have a Web site for your new business, you'll need a Web Host Provider (WHP) or Web Presence Provider (WPP) that will help you register your domain name, upload your site to their server, and setup mailboxes. If you don't already have a site, many host providers offer "starter kits" or basic Web site templates for developing your site and getting it up and running quickly. They also offer fee-based web development services from partner companies for personalized designs with more sophisticated features. The prices vary widely depending on the size, style, and functionality you prefer. For "do-it-yourselfers," software such as Microsoft Frontpage offers an application that's fast, easy to use, and supported by most host providers.

Remote collaboration

Will your work require collaboration with other team members or remote office locations? For collaboration and document sharing you should consider teleconferencing services that are available either through the Internet, such as WebEx, or through your local copy center such as Kinkos. Prices vary from free document annotation and read-only sharing to fee-based application and desktop sharing with streaming audio and video. Other collaboration options gaining in popularity are peer-to-peer networks such as Groove Networks (*www.groovenetworks.com*) that allow a secure method of collaborating with your clients behind firewalls.

Software utilities

Now that you're on your own, without a systems administrator to worry about data security and virus protection, you'll need to protect your own system from unexpected crashes, hackers, and viruses. Data security is a concern with all businesses. Invest in a good backup system for your data such as a Zip or Jazz drive, tape backup, and portable hard drives using USB and FireWire technology. Another alternative is the virtual drive that lets you lease drive space to back up your data via the Internet using a provider such as Xdrive Technology (*www.xdrive.com*) or Drive-way (*www.driveway.com*). Zip drives are faster and more convenient for backing up data, but they don't contain the storage capacity of a tape drive. Tape drives, on the other hand, have a large storage capacity for backing up your entire system configuration in addition to your data, but they run slower than Zip drives depending on your system configuration and the amount of data you've stored. Usually, you would have to run a tape backup during off-hours, such as over the weekend or during the night, as it can take several hours. USB and FireWire external hard drives provide extremely fast data transfer and large storage capacity, but at a premium price when compared to Zip, Jazz, and tape backup systems. In any case, determine what you're exposure to a major crash would be and decide on the best backup tool for your situation. If you're simply backing up data, then take into account the time it would take to reload and reconfigure all your software applications, patches and updates, etc. vs. waiting for the tape drive to restore your complete configuration.

If most of your files are large graphics and multimedia files, then you should consider the portable hard drives for speed and convenience. Rewritable CD ROM and DVD drives provide another alternative for data backup and storage of large multimedia files.

Securing your network or computer system from external issues is another security concern. DSL, satellite, cable, and other newer modem technology where you're continually logged into the Internet present potential security threats to your system from hackers as long as your computer is turned on. You should consider personal firewall protection available through most antivirus software providers such as Norton and McAfee. There is also a host of rated firewall and virus protection freeware/shareware available through Ziff-Davis (*www.zdnet.com*, look under "downloads").

PC World and their online publication (*www.pcworld.com*) offer comprehensive critique and analysis of computer software hardware and peripheral equipment in each issue. Consult them for advice on the best values for your computer needs.

Remember to save your receipts for all business-related purchases of furniture and fixtures and equipment for tax deductions. If you've purchased the equipment within the last five to seven years, consult your accountant about deducting a portion of the depreciation expense on equipment that wasn't originally purchased for the business, but is now being used extensively by the business.

Services for the small business owner

Just as companies are outsourcing their services to you, there are a number of convenient avenues to which you can outsource everything from clerical and accounting services. Many of these services help free your valuable time to focus on revenue generating activity. Most service providers have Web sites from which you can outsource services directly from your desktop. For example, a number of copy centers offer print on demand for quantity printing or special format printing via the Internet. You may have to install a small application onto your computer. Most applications are available free on CD-ROM from the service provider and they are easy to run.

Check the sites of the major office supply retailers for additional small business services. Most also offer convenient shopping by creating your own customized lists for frequently ordered supplies. This saves a great deal of time thumbing through paper catalogs or searching their database to locate item numbers for supplies that come in 57 different varieties. As an added benefit, most office supply retailers also offer free shipping on orders over a certain dollar amount along with lines of credit, and special discounts.

The following list represents a sampling of sites that offer services to small businesses:

❖ *www.Allbusiness.com*: small business services community.

❖ *www.Buyerzone.com*: small business services community.

❖ *www.Office.com*: small business services community.

❖ *www.Officemax.com*: office supplies and business services.

❖ *www.Onvia.com*: small business services community.

❖ *www.Sbaonline.sba.gov*: U.S. Small Business Administration.

❖ *www.Staples.com*: office supplies and business services.

❖ *www.Toolkit.cch.com*: small business services community.

To search for more small business sites, try typing a combination of the words and phrases such as *"small business," "sole proprietor," "home based business," "home office and telecommuting," "SOHO and small office home office"* into a search engine.

Record Keeping

This is an area of business management that many freelancers and independent consultants find tedious and time-consuming, not to mention non-value added. Undoubtedly, it's boring and mundane compared to the challenge of your daily professional work; however, it's a necessary evil in running an efficient business operation and ensuring that you're paying adequate taxes on your income and taking deductions where appropriate. Until you reach a point where you can afford to hire an assistant, you'll have to bear the burden. Fortunately, there are a number of software products that help streamline this process and provide vital information to help you run your business more efficiently.

Start by investing in an accounting software package for small businesses such as Quickbooks, Quickbooks Professional, or Peachtree Accounting. Some of these programs, such as Quicken, will integrate with certain contact management applications, such as Microsoft Outlook, making it faster and easier to share contact information between the two applications. These programs not only help you manage the billing and collections processes, but also let you create proposals and job estimates.

Usually, the software is easy to set up and relies on certain input from you, such as the type of business (what products and services your business offers), accounting method (cash versus accrual), and other expenses (equity or income accounts that you may wish to set up in addition to the pre-configured accounts that are included with the software). You must decide on an accounting method because the IRS requires that you to establish a single method for reporting your income and you must use that method consistently. Cash method means that you report the income at the point you are paid and accrual method is based on reporting the income at the point the order is booked. Consult your accountant or tax professional to help you determine the best method for your business.

You'll also need to have an idea of your rates or fees for the types of services you offer because you'll have to enter these into the system. When setting up your income accounts, try to keep in mind the type of information you'll want to receive in the reporting area. For example, if you're a marketing consultant, you might want to create broad categories for items such as branding, corporate image, market research, public relations, etc. under which you would include specific services offered in each area. Breaking down categories helps you track the types of services that are providing the most income. This part can be time-consuming, but, it's well worth it when you consider the valuable business information it will provide to help you determine how to allocate your marketing dollars among other important business decisions.

The same applies to setting up your unique expense categories. Consider how you would like to see the information reported and break down each expense category more specifically to help you better track that item. For example, if you spend a lot of time commuting between clients, you may wish to break down your travel expenses category into public transportation versus air travel. This will not only help you control your costs, but also provide more accurate proposals.

Setting up the software to suit your individual business needs can take a little extra time up front. However, the convenience of accurate, ready-to-use information can be well worth the initial time investment. Often, it's easier to set up your accounts correctly from the start than to modify them midway through the year.

Provided you've maintained accurate, up-to-date information, your accounting software will help you and your accountant save time in preparing and filing your tax returns. Many accountants will even work from an electronic file provided by your accounting software.

Another important element in record keeping is maintaining a current paper file of receipts for all your business expenses. Your paper file system can be as simple as an expander file or as elaborate as a metal file cabinet separated by months and then by categories within each month. In any case, you'll need an easy way to store the month's expense receipts and if necessary, broken down by category. Think in terms of an IRS audit. In the event of an audit, you'll be better prepared if your receipts are organized in monthly order as opposed to haphazardly thrown into a shoebox.

Your computer files are another important area to organize. Does your file system look like the equivalent of an electronic shoebox full of "stuff"? Organize your electronic files to make data easier to find and more efficient to back up. Create a folder for each client where you'll keep that client's electronic documentation, such as proposals, general correspondence, and project files. Most contact management programs allow you to link files to a specific contact so you'll have a running history of correspondence with the client, including e-mail. In the same way, you should also set up a hardcopy file system for contracts and other non-electronic documentation pertaining to each client.

If you are also working through agencies, keep all agency-related documentation in a file similar to your clients' files and remember to also keep accurate time records in an automated program such as Timeslips (*www.timeslips.com*). It will make it easier to verify that your compensation matches the hours you've worked and will keep track of hours accrued so that you can easily determine your eligibility for benefits. Most spreadsheet and some word processing programs offer templates for time tracking. If they're not already installed with your system, they may reside on the software application's installation CD or on the software company's Web site.

Time Management

Time management is topic about which tomes have been written, which is a testament to the importance of the topic—especially for the independent consultant. Yet it's an area that continues to elude many would-be successful permanent temps. The challenge is to develop the self-discipline to effectively manage your time and productivity.

Time management is all about making the most productive use of your time each day. Productivity isn't just about putting out more work. It's also about reducing the clutter or inefficiency that reduces your throughput. Making the most productive use of your time can mean scheduling 30 minutes downtime each day to help you refresh and avoid burnout. It can also mean parallel tasking (completing several tasks at the same time) to increase available time.

In order to effectively manage your time, you should consider a time management tool such as a DayTimer, Franklin Planner, a personal digital assistant (PDA), or personal information manager (PIM) accompanied by a software application. Note that both DayTimer and Franklin have software programs that synchronize with certain PDAs. Most PDAs, such as the Palm, Handspring, Psion, HP Jornada, Compaq, etc. will synchronize with your laptop and/or your desktop computer's contact management

and scheduling software. Some PDAs are based on the Palm operating system while others use Microsoft's Windows CE, an ab-
breviated form of Windows.

Regardless of the method you choose, *everything*, should go
into your scheduler. Whether it's business related or personal,
your scheduler maps your time and tracks expenses so that you
can effectively manage your business. Without a comprehensive
view of all of your time, you will quickly find yourself behind the
eight ball. You've probably heard this analogy a hundred times,
but it bears repeating. Managing your time is like planning a trip
across the country. You map your starting point, destination point,
and plan the route between the two points. Without the plan,
you'll wander aimlessly—never quite knowing where you're
headed. The same holds true in time management. Everyone has
the same amount of time each day, but how we plan and manage
our time determines whether or not we accomplish what we in-
tend to do.

For many busy permanent temps, daily scheduling and "to-
do" lists aren't enough. You'll need to look at larger blocks of
time such as weeks or even months and take into account the
percentage of your time allocated for each project. That's not to
say that you shouldn't plan each day. It means that you should
always keep a macro view of your schedule in mind so that each
day's tasks support your overall plan and allow you to optimize
your available time for generating the revenue you need to succeed as a permanent temp. For example, you're currently on a
two-month assignment that's winding down (final three weeks)
and you're planning a two-week vacation immediately following
the completion of the assignment. Meanwhile, a client wants to
hire your for an assignment that you estimate will take two weeks
to complete but could potentially impact your current assignment
and vacation. By looking at a two to three-month window, you'll
be able to explore the following scenarios:

A. See if the customer can hold off for six weeks until
   after your vacation.

B. Assuming that your time allocation for the remaining three weeks of your current assignment is 60 percent, you could begin part of the new assignment before breaking for vacation, then complete it at 100 percent time allocation following your vacation—extending the project duration from two to nearly three weeks.

C. Sacrifice your vacation.

D. Subcontract the job to a colleague for a finder's fee.

Effective time management puts you in control of your time and allows you to maximize your work-life balance.

Other time management techniques include:

❖ Parallel tasks: combining several activities into one. For example, if you need to leave your office go to the post office, try to minimize time spent away from the office by also doing your banking, stopping at the drycleaner, filling your gas tank, etc.

❖ Avoid bottlenecks: prevent the little things from piling up and becoming huge time consumers. For example, if you have a few bookkeeping entries to make, do them as they occur instead of letting them accumulate to the point where you'll need to take a substantial amount of your productive time completing them. Chances are, they'll only take a few minutes to do, so schedule them for a time in the day when your creative energy dips and you need a diversion. Bottlenecks can also back you into a corner at a time when you need to focus on revenue generating activity, by forcing you to handle a situation that you've allowed to bottleneck.

❖ Maximize your peak energy levels: scheduling brain power intensive activities during your high energy time of day. Everyone has a time of day when they're most energetic and productive. Determine when your most productive hours are and schedule project work during those hours. During your "off-peak" hours, schedule the more mundane or less energy draining tasks such as book keeping, phone calls, filing, sorting through your mail, etc.

❖ Build slack into your schedule: this is a flexibility factor or time cushion that helps compensate for projects that extend beyond your original estimate. If you don't have a lot of experience estimating jobs, you should allow yourself a small cushion of time over and above what you think is adequate. It protects you from missing a deadline, or taking on more work before completing a current assignment by compensating for unforeseen delays. Be careful not to build in so much slack that your estimate is far longer than what would normally be expected. If you're unsure about the timing of a project, talk to a colleague or another consultant in your field to help you estimate an adequate amount of time to complete the project without overshooting your estimate.

❖ Break down each project into manageable segments: a large, overwhelming project can be easily tamed by breaking it down into logical, more manageable segments. By scheduling a completion date for each segment, you'll be encouraged by your progress as you complete each milestone and the project will seem less stressful.

❖ Level resource peaks: minimizing the effects of a "feast or famine" schedule. No matter how you plan, sometimes it seems like everything happens at once and you find yourself with too much work at the same time. Conversely, you'll go through slumps where you may wonder where your next job is coming from. This phenomenon is prevalent when starting your business and you haven't yet built a steady base, so you can't yet afford to turn down work. Leveling is a project management technique that adjusts time and/or resources to minimize the volume of peaks and slumps. Obviously, a slump requires more business to fill. The peaks require either more resources or more time. A partner or subcontractor is a resource who could help you reduce your load. The other alternative is to have your clients accept a later start date or longer project duration.

❖ Go with the flow: schedule tasks that require full concentration for days when you have uninterrupted blocks of time. For example, you're in the midst of preparing a major corporate tax return and your six-month dental cleaning pops up on your calendar. To avoid the distraction and lose the productive workflow, reschedule the appointment to another day. Then take control of your schedule, and make that day your "interruption day." Schedule other appointments such as a business luncheon, haircut, return a library book, etc. to prevent interruptions from creeping up and taking control of your schedule.

❖ Above all, minimize the amount of time you waste each day. Often, time is wasted unconsciously or perhaps even subconsciously. You can reduce wasted time by avoiding the following:

1. **Procrastination:** putting off the inevitable only serves to make matters worse. Focus on the benefits of completing the project albeit financial rewards, referral business, accolades, etc. Oftentimes it's simply a matter of getting started. Once begun, the job doesn't seem quite as dreadful.

2. **Frequenting your e-mail inbox:** better yet, set up junk mail filters and avoid the distraction of the incoming junk so you can focus on the 20 percent that really matters. Also avoid getting caught up in the humorous and inspirational messages from friends and family. They're fun to read, but time consuming. Save them for after hours.

3. **Getting sidetracked on the Internet:** more time is wasted with the good intention of getting pertinent information while on the Internet. The Internet's designed for distraction. What seems like a few minutes of clicking on hyperlink after hyperlink actually turns into over an hour of surfing. Set a deadline and hold yourself to it. If you don't find what you're looking for, then hold off until later—after you've identified a strategy for locating the information.

4.   **Social engagements during productive hours:** "doing lunch" with friends and colleagues is an important part of networking. However, make it a planned activity so that you'll account for it in your schedule. Keep social engagements to a minimum during your work hours.

Remember to ask yourself this question throughout the day, "Is this the most productive use of my time?" If you consistently answer *yes*, then you're on your way to top efficiency. If you answer *yes* part of the time, then list those items that take you away from revenue generating activity and determine what you might be able to outsource, eliminate, or reschedule to a time that has a smaller impact on your revenue generating potential.

10 Ways to Avoid Complacency

During downtime it's easy to become complacent. There are several ways to effectively use downtime to your advantage to help reduce the risk of complacency. The following suggestions will help you avoid complacency while bolstering your marketing efforts:

1.   Update your resume. Even though you think it's up to date, review it anyway. There is always room for improvement and downtime presents a perfect opportunity to fine tune your resume without the pressures of having to send it to a potential client or employer.

2.   While you're updating your resume, find at least two places to send your resume. It can be for advertised positions, a new agency, or a company that is looking for consultants.

3.   If you have a Web site, update it. We've all fallen into the trap of lacking the time to adequately update our Web sites. Well, during downtime, you don't have an excuse not to update it.

4.   Visit a few job boards and post your newly revised resume.

5. Write a series of direct mailers targeted at your market niches, obtain a mail list, and send one of them. Save the other two for future mailings.

6. Contact a few clients and ask them for referrals or testimonials if they were pleased with your work. (You should make this part of any assignment that you successfully complete.)

7. Write an article on a topic of interest in your specialty and seek to have it placed in a trade journal or association newsletter.

8. Attend a networking event such as a seminar, trade show, or take a course that either complements or augments your existing skills

9. Practice your personal deliverables statement by making a few cold calls to prospects.

10. Do something that recharges you. Take a walk in the park, attend a yoga class, read a good book, surf, or whatever you enjoy to revitalize you for your next assignment.

Housekeeping 101

Organizing yourself is a critical factor in your ability to manage your time effectively. Disorganization forces you to expend valuable time on non-value added activities such as searching for files, locating e-mails, tracking down business cards, etc.

Organize your files and archive or purge data regularly. This holds true for both paper and electronic files. For example, e-mail inboxes can overflow with e-mails that you never seem to get to despite good intentions. Information usually falls into three categories:

A: Top priority, important reference, or requires action.

B: Somewhat important and probably should save just in case.

C: Ranges anywhere from nice to know to totally useless information and should rarely, if ever, be saved.

Type A information should be acted upon and filed. Type B information should be filed and if not acted upon within a reasonable amount of time, discarded. Typical B information includes e-mail newsletters, direct mails for conferences you would like to attend, and magazines that you put away for later reading. If you don't get to them later, then discard them, especially if subsequent issues begin arriving. You should touch type B information only once. The more you touch it, the more time and energy you waste contemplating what to do with it. Finally, type C information should simply be deleted, discarded, or otherwise permanently removed. It's quite liberating to wipe out a string of 20 or 30 useless emails in a single click.

E-mail is an area that can easily grow out of control. Most e-mail applications come with utilities to filter incoming mail based on the parameters that you establish, such as a junk mail filter for incoming messages with phrases like "save money now" or "lose weight fast." You can opt to have these messages automatically deleted or moved to a special folder that lets you quickly delete them all simultaneously. Remember to purge your deleted e-mail folder regularly as it can grow exponentially.

E-mail applications also provide a variety of ways to organize your messages and give you the ability to set up your own files. Although it can take some time, familiarize yourself with your e-mail program so that you can take advantage of the many built-in features for streamlining the handling of e-mail.

Contact Management

Ask any successful sales person what their most valuable asset is and they'll likely say their contacts. Managing your contacts and staying in touch with them is essential to ensuring repeat business and obtaining referral business. There are a number of contact management programs available such as Act!, Goldmine, and Contact Plus. If you're a Microsoft Office user, Outlook or Access will effectively manage your contacts. Most are easy to use and have a utility that lets you import your contact information from other electronic formats to avoid retyping information. If you're going from a paper file to an electronic file, then it might be worth your while to hire a typing whiz to quickly enter your data.

Similar to setting up your accounting software, you should keep in mind your reporting needs when entering information so that the appropriate fields are included in addition to the most basic fields of name, address, telephone number, etc. For example, if you're a legal consultant specializing in telecommunications contracts, among other contract specialties such as employment contracts, you'll probably want to add a field for "contract type" and/or "industry." This allows you to sort or filter your database to more accurately target specific market segments.

Keep a running history of your contact activity such as telephone conversations and project notes. The history makes it easier to respond to your clients' and prospects' specific needs and helps ensure accurate proposals. Most contact management programs allow you to attach or associate other files with the contact such as letters and e-mails for a comprehensive history.

Contact management programs come in a range of prices with a variety of features. Get the package that best suits your needs and your budget. If you're currently using the Microsoft Office Suite, you can simply use Outlook for both contact and time management or set up your contacts using Access. Whatever application you select, the databases can usually be imported/exported between the different applications.

Remember, your contact list is a valuable asset. Keeping it current in a database program is a good way to safeguard your contacts.

Customer Satisfaction

One of the best ways to ensure future jobs is to provide excellent service to existing clients. Whether you're working direct or through an agency, quality work, on-time/on-budget deliverables, and a professional demeanor go a long way to satisfying customers and ensuring repeat business.

The following are a few business basics that you should keep in mind when working with clients.

❖ Always return client calls and e-mails promptly—preferably within the same business day. At times this may not be possible, so you'll want to reach them as soon as possible the next business day. Determine a regular schedule for checking your messages. You may even want to setup incoming e-mail rules that prioritize key clients' e-mails in a special folder for fast, easy access.

❖ Deliver on-time and on-budget work. Nothing speaks to your credibility more than keeping your word. Remember, the purpose of hiring you is to fill a gap and speed progress.

❖ Know your clients' preferences—likes and dislikes. This information should be included in your client database and referred to when the client calls.

❖ Keep your clients informed. If you're planning to take a vacation, let your clients know if you'll be unavailable. This is another way to stay in touch with them.

❖ Make it easy for clients to do business with you. Simple ideas such as placing your phone, fax, and e-mail information on all documentation make it easier for customers to reach you. Customizing a template that's consistent with what your client uses streamlines work on their end and is another way to make it easy for clients to do business with you.

❖ Always send a thank you note to clients and ask them for referrals.

❖ Handle conflicts with professionalism. Listen carefully, respect the client's viewpoint, calmly interject your viewpoint, and attempt a win-win solution.

In consulting, the majority of your business will come from repeat clients, and the only way to harness repeat business is to keep your clients satisfied.

Summary

Working as a free agent requires a great deal of self-discipline. Maintaining a well-organized office environment with all the necessary conveniences helps ensure peak efficiency and frees you from the time-wasting clutter. Vehemently manage your time to optimize customer satisfaction, income, and to prevent burnout. Good organization and time management skills will help you avoid sabotaging your success as a permanent temp.

Key points:

❖ Maintain a comfortable office environment with convenience features that save time and increase your throughput.

❖ Get as much computing power as you can afford that will also meet your current and projected needs.

❖ Protect your computer data from hackers, viruses, and unforeseen crashes with personal firewall and anti-virus software and backup utilities.

❖ Rely on small business resources to help you become more efficient.

❖ Keep current and accurate paper and electronic records.

❖ Make the most productive use of your time each day and use available time management tools such as PDAs, PIMs, and other organizers to simplify the task.

❖ Know what wastes your time each day and do your best to minimize it.

❖ Keep paper files organized by purging unnecessary information regularly. Similarly, avoid "digital disarray" and organize your electronic files, regularly purging unnecessary information.

❖ Ensuring new and repeat business is partly associated with good contact management and customer satisfaction. Make it easy for your customers to do business with you.

❖ Keep your promises to your clients by delivering on-time and on-budget projects.

Action Plan

1. Make a list of all the essential office items you'll need using the items mentioned in this chapter as a guide. Remember to check the Internet for good deals on office and computer equipment and supplies.

2. Take a look at your office setup to determine if it's comfortable and designed for peak efficiency (i.e. is your phone on or near your desk or on the other side of the room?).

3. Create templates for the business forms you'll need.

4. Purchase or update anti-virus software for the latest virus protection.

5. Obtain a computer backup system for your data.

6. Obtain a software accounting package designed for the small business and keep your records up to date.

7. Set up organized paper and electronic file systems.

8. If you already have an established file system, go through it and purge any unnecessary data.

9. Purchase a time management tool and use it regularly, even if it is a little uncomfortable at first. When you first begin using your time management tool, it may seem like it takes more time to use; however, that feeling goes away after you've become accustomed to using it.

10. Make a list of the top distractions that take you away from productive work. Determine which of those distractions can be eliminated, minimized, or managed.

11. Enter your contacts and clients into a contact management program and keep it current.

Can I Make Money at It?

If you have a goal in mind and you know what you'll need to achieve that goal, chances are, you'll succeed. In this chapter, we'll take a look at the financial implications of becoming a permanent temp and how best to prepare yourself for financial success as a permanent temp. This chapter is designed to provide a guide and perhaps even raise additional questions about the financial aspects of becoming a permanent temp, though it's not a substitute for professional advice from an accountant or financial planner.

Can I Afford to Be a Permanent Temp?

First, you'll need to do a personal and professional financial self-assessment. It's important to determine your ability to cover both your personal and professional expenses so that you not only have food, clothing, and shelter, but also the means to work and promote your business. If you are only covering your personal expenses, then you will lose money when you consider the costs of being self-employed, such as healthcare insurance, disability, retirement planning, etc. However, if at the beginning of the book your goal in becoming a permanent temp was to provide a small side income while continuing a full-time job or during your retirement, the business financial implications may not apply.

Personal financial self-assessment

What are your personal monthly costs? Break down your costs into the following categories:

1. Fixed spending: mortgage, rent, utilities, etc.

2. Variable spending: food, clothing, commuting, etc.

3. Discretionary spending: entertainment, etc.

Prioritize your discretionary spending to determine where you might be able to reduce expenses. For example, do you need to spend the additional $50 per month for premium cable channels or will one premium channel do? Are you eating out every night when it might be less expensive to buy groceries and eat in?

Prioritize any tradeoffs, taking into consideration independence, flexibility, and control over your schedule. Then ask yourself: will you incur any real expenses being independent versus being an employee? Will your agency or employers take on expenses or will you need front money, such as a retainer? Most experts agree that you should have at least a four to six month cushion before leaving a full-time position to become an independent consultant.

Professional financial self-assessment

Perform an analysis of the cash flow cushion required to go into the area you're considering. What is the assignment time lag? Do you expect a long duration between assignments? What is the initial financial expectation for your specialty? Determine your hourly rate or project fees necessary to meet your expenses and remember to include healthcare and retirement planning.

With a rough idea of your financial picture, you'll immediately know if the intake can meet your required personal outlay. If yes, then it's time to take a closer look at the business operation costs of becoming a permanent temp.

Marketing Costs

If you're not planning to sign with an agency, you'll need to plan for marketing expenses. Typical expenses include postage, list rental, fulfillment, space advertising, Web site hosting, and production costs for the design and printing of sales brochures.

These costs vary based on the extent of the program. Mail lists can range from $100 per 1,000 names to more than $700 per thousand names for a minimum of 5,000 names. The cost is dependent on the type of list (business list versus consumer) and user selectable variables such as phone number, e-mail, etc. The volume is usually too large for an individual to mail and probably to respond to assuming your list and letter pull an average 3 percent to 5 percent response. You'll most likely want to subcontract this service to a fulfillment company for an additional fee.

Space and banner advertisements vary significantly. Check with the publication or Web site for rates. Rates are based on size of the ad for print media and frequency of insertions. Plan on at least a small text ad in the classified section of trade journals for a range of about $75 to $500. Many online publications offer monthly rates to link to your Web site.

If you plan on developing a Web site, allow for domain registration, usually around $70 for two years, and web host provider fees that can range from free to more than $100 per month depending on any optional services you select. Several companies offer preformatted templates that allow you to quickly create a site, but you can pay a design firm to create your site or you can buy a software package and do it yourself.

There are a number of other incidental marketing expenses to consider that are minimal in cost but add to your incremental start-up marketing expenses. You'll need a small supply of letterhead envelopes and business cards. Because the majority of correspondence is electronic, you can easily design stationery and business cards and then print them on demand. If you plan on telemarketing, you'll need to allow for an increase in your long distance phone bill.

Remember, effective marketing programs must be ongoing. That is, you can't stop marketing yourself while you have business or you'll have no future business once the project is complete. This is one of the most difficult and easily overlooked aspects of being independent. You must keep a steady stream of leads in your database to ensure ongoing future business. At times, this can present a predicament because sometimes several clients require your services simultaneously. Should you be lucky enough to find yourself in this situation, if some of your clients cannot wait, it is always best to refer them to a trusted colleague. Clients would rather be referred elsewhere than miss their target delivery date because you've taken on more than your time permits. Another alternative would be to take the job and manage the project with your trusted colleague as a subcontractor.

Healthcare Insurance

If you're currently a full-time employee and your employer provids group health insurance benefits, you should be eligible for COBRA (Consolidated Omnibus Budget Reconciliation Act of 1985), an extension of your existing healthcare benefits for up to 18 months. You will need to notify your existing employer of your desire to participate within 60 days and you will be responsible for paying the premium, which may include an additional small administration fee. If COBRA doesn't apply, then you may be able to convert your employer's group policy into an individual policy.

Another option is to consider health coverage through an agency or industry association. If you think you'll experience a lapse in coverage during the transition, you can obtain a short-term policy (duration of two to six months) that will provide minimum coverage in the interim. For example, when working with an agency, you may need to accrue a certain number of hours before becoming eligible for healthcare benefits, so you'll want to consider a short-term policy to cover the duration while accruing hours.

For access to hundreds of insurance companies and rates, visit the following sites:

- ❖ *www.insweb.com.*
- ❖ *www.insuremarket.com* (formerly Quicken InsureMarket).
- ❖ *www.quotesmith*.com.

Also check specific industry associations Web sites that offer benefits to qualified members such as Independent Computer Consultants Association (ICAA).

Types of healthcare plans

The two most common healthcare plans include fee-for-service and managed care. The fee-for-service plan price structure is based on deductibles versus premiums—in other words, the higher the deductible, the lower the premium, and vice versa. Generally, the reimbursement is based on the 80/20 principle, although some policies offer 70/30 and even 60/40. The doctor is reimbursed 80 percent of reasonable and customary charges and you're responsible for 20 percent plus any amount over and above the reasonable and customary fee. You can choose the doctor you wish to see. There are usually out-of-pocket maximums as well as lifetime limits.

Managed care programs include health maintenance organizations (HMOs), preferred provider organizations (PPOs), and point-of-service (POS) plans. You pay a monthly or quarterly premium and use the participating healthcare providers. There are usually $5 and $10 copayments for prescriptions and office visits. You'll need to obtain a participating primary care physician from whom you'll obtain referrals to participating specialists.

PPOs and POSs are a combination of fee-for-service and HMOs. You can select any participating physician and go to any specialist without a referral. As long as you see participating physicians, you'll only be responsible for your copay like a typical HMO. Should you go outside of the plan, the plan will reimburse the physician 80 percent and you'll be responsible for 20 percent like a fee-for-service plan.

Medical Savings Accounts (MSAs)

Medical savings accounts are tax-exempt custodial accounts that allow you to contribute money for future medical expenses. Offered as a "pilot program" during the year 2000, perhaps it will be available on a broader scope in the future.

MSAs are designed for the self-employed or employees of small businesses (50 or fewer employees) who have a high deductible health plan (HDHP) and no other healthcare coverage. If you are unable to obtain a group policy or join a managed care program, you may be eligible to establish a medical savings account.

MSAs are available through a financial institution or insurance company. You must meet the following eligibility requirements to open an MSA:

1. Be self-employed or work for a small employer (50 or fewer employees).

2. Have an HDHP. HDHPs are health plans which have a higher deductible than most typical health plans and the maximum deductible limits are also fairly high. IRS Publication 969, *Medical Savings Accounts (MSAs)* describes the details of eligibility, HDHP deductible limits, contribution limits, setting up, and managing the account.

Unlike traditional tax-deferred contributions to a medical plan, contributions made to an MSA remain in the account each year until you use them. Interest on the amount in the account is tax-free and contributions are tax deductible. Any medical expenses not reimbursed by your HDHP are reimbursed through distributions from your MSA.

Check with your accountant and read IRS Publication 969, *Medical Savings Accounts (MSAs)* at *www.irs.gov/prod/forms_pubs/pubs/p969toc*.htm.

The following Web sites are very informative and will help you know what to ask as you research healthcare insurance. Visit:

❖ *www.ahcpr.g*ov (Agency for Healthcare Research and Quality).

❖ *www.healthfinder.org* (U.S. Department of Health and Human Services Web site).

❖ *www.hiaa.org* (Health Insurance Association of America).

What does it cost?

Healthcare plans vary widely in coverage, premiums, deductibles, coinsurance, and copay amounts. You really need to determine your needs, and then obtain a quote. Many insurance Web sites offer the ability to obtain a quote by completing an online form. (The same holds true for disability and liability insurance.)

The following amounts are general and for planning purposes only. Discuss your needs with an insurance agent for the most accurate rates based on coverage.

COBRA can range from $200 per month for individual coverage to $400 or $500 per month for family coverage.

Group rates for medical start at around $250 per month for individual coverage. Family coverage and rates obtained outside of a group are substantially higher. The premiums vary based on the following:

1. Type of plan (i.e. fee-for-service, managed care such as HMO, PPO, or POS).

2. Deductible, coinsurance, and maximum out-of-pocket limits.

3. Additional programs such as long term care, emergency care, etc.

4. Your geographic location.

Remember, medical and dental expenses in excess of 7.5 percent of your adjusted gross income are tax deductible. See your accountant for the best way to treat these types of deductions.

Individual insurance

The healthcare benefits previously described are available on an individual basis. The fee is higher for individual policies so you will need to carefully review the policies and select the best value for the coverage you need. To help minimize your premiums, consider a group plan through an agency or industry association.

Disability

Disability insurance protects you from unforeseen medical issues that may prevent you from working and prevents loss of income while you're incapacitated. Disability is critical if you're not covered by an agency policy or if you're an independent.

If you're self-employed and injured on the job, you cannot file with the state for workers' compensation, so disability insurance is essential to protecting your ability to continue receiving an income.

Even though you may have long-term disability insurance, you may also wish to consider a short-term disability policy to avoid delays sometimes associated with obtaining your long-term disability benefits while your case is under review. Short-term disability avoids having to go without income for a two or three month period.

General Liability Insurance

If you're an independent contractor not affiliated with an agency, companies may ask, "Do you have a certificate of insurance?" They are referring to general liability insurance for "errors and omissions" that you would carry to protect yourself from the unlikely event of injury due to an accident while on the company's premises. It protects the company from being sued by you in the event of an accident on their premises, such as falling in the company's parking lot and breaking your arm. General liability insurance requirements vary from state to state.

Professional liability

Professional liability protects you from financial loss in the event your services cause the company to incur a loss. It protects you from a hefty, financially damaging lawsuit. For example, you build a retail commerce site that crashes every hour, forcing an unhappy client to wage a lawsuit against you. Limits of liability can be set to a specific amount depending on your profession's risk factor. Many independent contractors and agency agreements limit the liability to a fixed amount such as the last three months of what you were paid to work there.

Professional liability insurance can be a very costly proposition. Check with an insurance agent and legal professional regarding the need to carry professional liability insurance and if necessary, the recommended amount.

What does it cost?

Long-term disability varies according to the amount of coverage you select. Plans start at approximately $150 per month for minimal coverage. You'll need to determine your lost income per month should you become ill for an extended period of time. At least determine the amount needed to cover your expenses for an extended period without regular income. That will give you an idea of how much coverage you'll need.

General liability insurance starts at around $50 to $75 per month but varies significantly depending on the amount of coverage and your exposure to liability.

Tax and Retirement Considerations

As an independent contractor or sole proprietor, you'll need to be aware of various tax considerations when becoming a permanent temp, especially when working independent of an agency. Although this section raises important considerations regarding tax planning, it is not a substitute for the professional advice of an accountant or financial planner.

Estimated quarterly taxes

Most full-time employees or consultants/contractors who maintain employer of record status with an agency (W2s) pay their taxes through withholding. However, if you're not affiliated with an agency or you've earned income as a 1099 in addition to that from the agency, you'll have to pay estimated tax on the net income earned as a 1099 if you anticipate owing at least $1,000 in taxes. You'll calculate and report your estimated tax using IRS Form 1040 ES. Failure to pay estimated quarterly taxes could subject you to a penalty. Payments are due the 15th of April, June, September, and in January of the following year for calendar tax years.

See your accountant or visit the IRS Web site (Publication 505, *Tax Withholding and Estimated Tax*) *www.irs.gov/forms_pubs/pubs/p505ch02.htm* for more information about estimating quarterly taxes.

Self-employment tax (SE)

The self-employment tax affects the self-employed or independent contractor without an employer of record and covers your Social Security. It's normally included as part of the withholding; however, because self-employed or independent contractors without employers of record do not have taxes withheld, you will need to include it as part of your estimated quarterly taxes.

According to IRS Publication 533, *Tax Withholding and Estimated Tax* (*www.irs.gov/forms_pubs/pubs/p533toc.htm*), the SE tax rate is 15.3 percent (12.4 percent social security tax plus 2.9 percent medicare) for net earnings from $400 up to $72,600. After that, various exceptions apply. Half of the SE tax is deductible when filing your taxes. It's best to talk to an accountant or visit the IRS Web site for additional information including the forms you'll need to file and any exemptions for which you may be eligible. Additional information can be found in IRS Publication 533, *Tax Withholding and Estimated Tax*, also available on the IRS Web site mentioned above.

Other tax reporting

If you subcontract any work, you will need to file form 1099-MISC. Subcontracted work includes payments for services provided to your business such as attorney and accountant fees or fees for services provided by subcontractor who are not employees.

Obtain more information about other miscellaneous returns in IRS publication 583, *Starting a Business and Keeping Records* under "Information Returns" at *www.irs.gov/forms_pubs/pubs/ p58307.htm.*

Incorporating or forming a partnership or limited liability corporation (LLC)

Although a sole proprietorship is easy to form, there are draw-backs such as the 15.3 percent SE tax and the fact that you have unlimited liability (your personal assets are not protected from creditors). Other options, such as forming a C or S corporation or a limited liability corporation, offer personal liability protection and are not subject to the 15.3 percent SE tax.

In a C corporation you would have to pay corporate taxes on profit and if dividends are paid, shareholders would also pay taxes on dividends. This is the so-called "double taxation." However, medical expenses are 100 percent deductible and, in certain cases, excluded from gross income of 50 percent of gains on the sale of qualified small business stock. See IRS Publication 550, *Investment Income and Expenses,* Chapter 4, Gains on Qualified Small Business Stock for additional information *(www.irs.gov/prod/ forms_pubs/pubs/p5500410.htm)*.

An S corporation on the other hand, avoids the double taxation because there is no corporate income tax. Instead, income and expenses are passed through to shareholders to report on their personal tax returns. To take advantage of the S corporation tax benefit, you must file IRS Form 2553 within 75 days of incorporating. Even C corporations can be treated as S corporations for tax purposes by timely filing Form 2553 and qualifying for S corporation status.

According to IRS Publication 550, *Investment Income and Expenses*, in order to qualify for S corporation status, you must meet the following guidelines:

1. It must be a domestic corporation.

2. It must have only one class of stock.

3. It must have no more than 75 shareholders. When counting shareholders, a husband and wife and their estates are treated as one shareholder.

4. Its shareholders must be only individuals, estates (including estates of individuals in bankruptcy), certain trusts, and certain tax-exempt organizations.

5. It cannot have any nonresident alien shareholders.

6. It cannot be a financial institution that uses the reserve method of accounting for bad debts. Certain other types of corporations also do not qualify.

7. All shareholders must agree to the corporation's decision to be an S corporation.

Tax returns for an S corporation are filed on form 1120S. Be aware that certain states and cities such as New York City, do not recognize S corporation tax status and treat S corporations like a C corporation. Check with your accountant or tax professional when filing your state returns.

A limited liability partnership is ideal if you want the pass through (taxes are passed through to shareholders as opposed to a corporate tax) tax advantages of an S corporation, but do not meet the criteria for becoming one. Also, your personal assets are protected in a limited liability partnership.

Tax deduction for business use of your home or apartment

Using an area of your home exclusively and regularly for conducting business may qualify you for a deduction. According to

IRS Publication 587, *Business Use of Your Home (www.irs.gov/ forms_pubs/pubs/p587toc.htm)* you may qualify for deduction under the following guidelines:

1. Your use of the business part of your home must be:

   a. Exclusive.

   b. Regular.

   c. For your trade or business.

2. AND The business part of your home must be *one* of the following:

   a. Your principal place of business.

   b. A place where you meet or deal with patients, clients, or customers in the normal course of your trade or business.

   c. A separate structure (not attached to your home) you use in connection with your trade or business.

For example, if you conduct business in your kitchen and you or other family members also use the kitchen for meals, etc. it cannot be deducted. Use must be exclusive. Most independent consultants, who do not have separate offices, set aside an area in their house for exclusive business use. It can be part of a den or family room as long as it is used exclusively by you for conducting business.

If you qualify for the deduction, then determine the percentage of your home used for conducting business by dividing the area used for business by the total area of your home. For example, if you have a 2,500 square foot home and use a 200 square foot room as your office 200 divided by 2,500 equals .08 or 8 percent. However, you lose certain future tax benefits when you sell your home at a later date. Speak with an accountant or visit the IRS site for additional information on calculating deductions and determining deduction limits at *www.irs.gov/forms_pubs/pubs/ p587toc.htm.*

Tax deductions for business furniture and equipment

You may also be eligible to deduct expenses for certain equipment such as computers and peripheral equipment (phones, PDAs, etc.) for business use. Referred to as a section 179 deduction, it allows you to deduct all or part of the cost of this type of equipment as opposed to taking depreciation deductions over a specified period. There are, of course, certain limits and restrictions in taking a section 179 deduction that you should discuss with your accountant or learn more by reading IRS Publication 946, *How to Depreciate Property,* Chapter 2, "Section 179 Deduction" at *www.irs.gov/forms_pubs/pubs/p9460201.htm*.

You would use the section 179 deduction on items purchased and used for the business immediately after purchase. For example, if you decide to become a permanent temp today, you can't go through the prior year's expenses of computer equipment or other peripheral expenses that were for personal use at the time, but now will be used for your business. However, you may be eligible to deduct depreciation based on a specified recovery period—five or seven years depending on the type of equipment and the depreciation method applied. Your accountant can explain the appropriate depreciation method.

Tax deferred retirement savings

As a permanent temp, it's a good idea to plan for your retirement and take advantage of tax deferred savings programs such as individual retirement account (IRAs) which typically lower your taxable income making your tax burden a little lighter and providing a nest egg for your retirement. These may be offered through your agency; however, if you plan to remain independent, you can obtain these through the following:

- ❖ Banks and other financial institutions.
- ❖ Mutual fund or life insurance companies.

Consider setting up a simplified employee pension (SEP), which is ideal for sole proprietors. SEPs allow you to invest in your retirement via IRAs without the complexities of major corporate pension plans. Traditional IRAs are the financial instruments found in SEPs. A traditional IRA allows you to invest pretax dollars. Taxes are paid when you take distributions from your IRA, subject to certain restrictions and possible penalties.

As a self-employed permanent temp, you can contribute up to 15 percent of your self-employed net earnings up to a certain amount into a SEP. Because your deduction amount and your net earnings are dependent on each other, you'll have to adjust the rate to compensate for the difference. Consult with your accountant and refer to IRS publication 590, *Individual Retirement Arrangements*, Chapter 4, "Simple Employee Pensions (SEP)" at *www.irs.gov/forms_pubs/pubs/p5900402.htm.*

Another type of IRA is the Roth IRA. Unlike traditional IRAs, the Roth IRA does not reduce your taxable income up front and cannot be used in a SEP. Instead, qualified distributions from the Roth IRA become tax-free later pending certain time limits, age limits, and other restrictions. Check with your accountant to determine which IRA is most advantageous to your financial situation or read IRS Publication 590, *Individual Retirement Arrangements*, Chapter 2, "Roth IRAs" at *www.irs.gov/forms_pubs/pubs/p590ch02.htm.*

Cost of Downtime

When making the decision to become a permanent temp, you'll need to compensate for downtime between assignments. If your goal is to generate an annual income equal to that of your full-time salary, then you'll need to compensate by adjusting your rate accordingly or ensure that downtime is minimal.

To determine the cost of downtime, use the following formula:

$$S \div WD = DR$$

Where: S = salary

WD = working days (use 235: typical amount used in the consulting industry including sick/personal time and a factored downtime for the agency to locate your next position)

DR = daily rate

For example, if you have an annual salary of $100,000, then:
$$\$100,000 \div 235 = \$425$$
You earn $425 per day for 235 days.

That amount includes employer-paid benefits such medical, dental, and long-term disability. So as a permanent temp responsible for your own insurance, you'll have to earn more than $425 per working day to earn the same $100,000.

Let's assume that as a 1099 permanent temp, your combined medical (individual coverage), dental (individual coverage), long-term disability, and general liability insurance cost $10,000 per year.
$$\$10,000 \div 235 = \$43 \text{ per working day}$$
Your insurance costs are $43 per working day.

When you deduct these expenses from your $425 daily rate ($425 – $43 = $382), you'll see that your net income is reduced to about $90,000 ($382 × 235). To make up for the $10,000 shortfall, you would have to work an additional 26 days ($382 × 26 = $10,000 *rounded*) or 261 working days (235 + 26) to increase your daily rate by $43.

If you're fortunate and have enough business to keep you working at your desired rate for 261 days, then you'll meet your $100,000 goal. That may not be the case when starting out. You'll have to allow for downtime between projects, any vacation you're planning to take, and time to market the business.

Another way of estimating a comparable rate is to determine your load for operating the business. Use the following approximate percentages of your $100,000 salary to determine the load.

Taxes	13 percent
Health Insurance	10 percent
Office, car, and other business expenses	15 percent
Vacation	2 percent
Total load:	40 percent

Then multiply your annual salary by 1.4 (estimated load from above) and divide by the number of working days, or 235 (from the previous example), to arrive at your daily rate.

For example:

$$\$100,000 \times 1.4 = \$140,000$$

$$\$140,000 \div 235 = \$595 \text{ daily rate}$$

If you're still not sure whether to sign with an agency (W2 tax status) or go it alone (1099 or corp to corp tax status), determine the value of your downtime (idle time between assignments). Compare that figure to your rate with an agency. If you think an agency would assign you to more opportunities than you could find on your own, it may be worth it to try an agency. However, if you have the right contacts, the marketing savvy, and a means to locate opportunities, you may find that you can earn more money as an independent.

Summary

Becoming a permanent temp requires an in-depth look at your financial picture. Your analysis should include more that just looking at your revenue potential, but a look at your *profitability* potential. Your profitability potential depends on the amount of additional business expenses you plan to incur to cover healthcare, disability, and liability insurance, plus your retirement planning. If you're not planning to work through an agency, then allow for marketing expenses.

Becoming a permanent temp impacts your tax situation too. It's important to know how to establish your business and understand the tax ramifications of your setup. Consult an accountant or tax professional for the best advice on starting your business. With a clear understanding of your financial picture, you'll be able to determine the best way to achieve financial satisfaction as a permanent temp.

Key points

❖ Before you "quit you day job," you'll need to estimate your expenses to determine the income you'll need to cover both your personal and business expenses.

❖ Determine your business structure (sole proprietor, S corporation, or limited liability corporation) keeping in mind the tax advantages, liability issues, and criteria for becoming an S corporation.

❖ As a sole proprietor, you will need to make quarterly tax payments.

❖ Carefully research insurance plans to find the coverage you need at a price you can afford.

❖ Consider disability insurance to protect you from unforeseen situations that could adversely affect your income and, ultimately, your ability to meet expenses.

❖ Consider starting a tax deferred savings program for your retirement.

❖ Check with an industry association or other related trade associations for potential savings on group healthcare and insurance benefits.

❖ Remember to consider downtime when estimating your income.

Action Plan

Given the various insurance, tax, and marketing considerations, you're now ready to visit an accountant, tax, or financial planner. It's a good idea to prepare a brief business plan with estimated monthly gross revenue to help your accountant advise on the best type of business to establish.

1. Determine the type of business setup most suitable to your unique financial situation.

2. Take a few days to visit your preferred insurance sites and obtain quotes on health, dental, disability, and general liability insurance. Compare notes with other independents.

3. Develop a marketing plan that includes who you can contact in your immediate circle (warm market), contacts from former affiliations, and a method for reaching them.

4. Estimate the cost of reaching prospects.

5. Using the hourly rate information from Chapter 4, *Compensation*, estimate the annual income needed to operate profitably.

6. Using the equations in this chapter, determine how many assignments you'll need to reach your income projections.

Confessions of a Permanent Temp

Despite the research and time that went into writing this book, there's no substitute for real live information from actual permanent temps. These real temps offer humor, advice, and an overall sense of what it's really like to be a permanent temp. The following advice comes from several sources: personal interviews, RealRates.com bulletin board, and Freelance Online, Ltd. bulletin board.

If this chapter doesn't scare you away from pursuing a permanent temping career, all the best as you embark on the future of employment opportunities.

We discussed interviewing techniques in Chapter 3. In this first example, the consultant recalls a rather peculiar interview.

> I was asked, "Do you prefer to be called David or Dave?"
> I replied that either was acceptable, to which I was told,
> "Really, you must prefer one or the other, which is it?"
> This exchange went back and forth several times, until I
> realized that this was going nowhere and the HR person
> was not going to let go of it. So I cheerfully said, "[C]all

me Bert." Huh?? was the response I got from the interviewer. We continued on, and I never was offered the position, or the courtesy of a return phone call. This, after I passed the day-long video taping of the role-playing "test." Hmmm. I think it worked out for the better.

Chapter 2 discusses the pros and cons of seeking work through agencies. The following temp obviously had a bad agency experience.

Be weary of the honest and seemingly ethical brokers as they often end up being the sleaziest of them all which you will find out in time.

Chapter 8 provided information on what to charge for your services. The following rate advice is a common area of concern for the novice consultant. This information was provided by a 10-year veteran of the freelance lifestyle.

Your total hourly rate is what you need to charge per hour on all the hours you expect to bill in a year in order to earn the gross income it will take to pay yourself the salary you want to earn, cover all the expenses of running your business, put something away for your retirement, and show a profit in your business. This means having a target income in mind, predicting your expenses, and forecasting how many hours you're going to bill. All of which is pretty difficult for a lot of freelancers to do.

The shortcut method—and which seems to produce the same hourly rate as more complex calculations—is to start with a gross salary, add 33% to 50% (or more) for expenses and profit, and divide by 1,000. The answer is your hourly rate.

The numbers you plug in to any formula will certainly increase over time. But the basic formula won't.

Good luck,

Ken Norkin

Ken Norkin is a fulltime freelance copywriter, creative director, and consultant specializing in business-to-business marketing communications. Ken is about to celebrate the 10th anniversary of his freelance business, KN Creative.

We discussed agency agreements and employment contracts in Chapter 5. The following free agent found herself in a quandary over a noncompete clause with an interesting twist.

I've searched the archives and Web for this info & have found good info on noncompete agreements in general, but nothing on this twist. I work half-time (W-2) for a company that provides content for instructional Internet sites. I'm also building a freelance business doing similar work, without stepping on toes. I haven't signed a noncompete with my employer. They have no problem with my freelance work, and several other workers also freelance.

However, my boss is about to sign a contract with a major Internet site. According to the boss (I haven't seen it yet), the contract says that no employee on the project will do work for the clients' competitors now or in the future. My boss has gotten them to narrow down the time & other constraints, but the fact remains that he will sign a contract that says I can't do a big chunk of my freelance work.

The contract doesn't limit just our company's actions. It wants to limit the work of individual employees. It seems bizarre that my employer could sign a noncompete agreement in my name. I'm not personally going to sign anything. Is this enforceable? By agreeing to employment, have I also agreed to any contract my employer signs regarding my individual outside work and future employment?

The following reply to the aforementioned noncompete quandary comes from another freelancer.

Your employer signing a contract that says his company and employees will not work for the client's competitors probably does not bind you to the terms of that contract.

Your boss has put himself in a position where he has only two ways to live up to the terms of the contract: (1) get all employees to sign a similar noncompete agreement; (2) issue a policy statement that says that as of such-and-so date it is the policy of ThisCompany that no employee, during his or her employment with ThisCompany, may also work for any competitor of This-Company or its clients.

I think the signed noncompete, especially applying to actual employees, will be enforceable if it does not have unreasonable or open-ended time limits (which courts have routinely frowned on).

The unilateral company policy statement may or may not be enforceable.

But he's got to try something.

You, on the other hand, should probably do what you want until and unless asked to stop. That's when you'll need to decide whether to comply, quit, or fight.

The topic of disability insurance was covered in Chapter 8 and the following useful advice was supplied by Janet Ruhl.

Once there is anything questionable on your health history, you will not be able to get disability insurance. So the time to buy it is while you are healthy and can't imagine needing it. I have personally encountered people who were totally disabled in their late 20s and early 30s and reduced to living on welfare because they did not have this kind of coverage. It could happen to anyone due to a self-caused auto accident or a progressive neuromuscular disease like Multiple Sclerosis (which is rarer among men, but not unknown—and when it hits men, BTW, is much more destructive and fast moving than when it hits women).

Taxes, covered in Chapter 8, are an important consideration for the permanent temp. The following examples provide good advice on how to handle taxes.

It was great; I had received several gigs and had $10,000 in my checking account. "This freelancing is pretty nice," I thought to myself. Then it hit me; there's no employer withholding taxes or paying part of the Social Security and Medicare. Plus I had to pay quarterly taxes for which I had missed the first two filing deadlines. In the end, I had to pay three quarters including the 15.3% Social Security and Medicare taxes, which left me with less than $3,000 in my account. The moral of the story is: "Keep your books in order and stay current on your quarterly tax payments[.]"

The next post, provided by "Dinosaur," offers more good tax advice.

Get your stuff together and keep it that way on an annual basis.

Once a year, see your tax lawyer/CPA and go over your returns.

That way, if you are audited, your tax lawyer/CPA has a fighting chance to get you off clean.

In Chapter 7 we discussed how to "behave" like a permanent temp and avoid complacency. The following advice will help you avoid the sometimes lackadaisical attitude spawned by the home office environment.

In this example, a permanent temp was enjoying the home office culture of wearing robe and slippers to work. The extremely casual environment soon became a distraction in that he was unable to fully focus on the business. To shift to a more productive office mindset, he showered, dressed (real clothes, not robe and slippers) and walked around the block to get a cup of coffee. This 20-minute routine cleared his thoughts and better prepared him for a more productive day in the home office.

We discussed marketing yourself in Chapter 6. The next example shows what can happen when an overzealous permanent temp sells himself out of an assignment.

A novice temp was interviewing for a potential assignment. The interviewer asked the prospective permanent temp how to handle a particular technical issue. Eager to get the assignment, he prepared a white paper on the subject. The prospective client inquired about additional issues, to which the eager permanent temp responded. During the course of a follow-up call, the eager permanent temp learned that the prospective client not only cancelled the project, but also implemented the eager permanent temp's ideas. The eager permanent temp never had a chance to even quote, much less get paid for his consulting. The moral of the story is never give out too much information. The idea is to give the client a reason to want to hire you.

The following interesting anecdotes come from permanent temps who've found satisfaction in being their own bosses.

I love freelancing. In fact, it's been one year and my marketing efforts are starting to payoff in additional business and referrals. I don't want to work 40 hours a week for someone else.

And finally...

Being independent is the way to go. In fact, my worst day contracting was better than my best day in the corporate world.

Frequently Asked Questions About Permanent Temping

How can I determine if my prospective agency is effective?

First, visit their Web site and look for information on the amount of jobs posted in your field. They may indicate how many placements they make in a certain period of time. Visit other HR or job-related sites and see if they advertise. Remember, your agency should be investing in marketing to drive clients to their Web site. In cases where the agency is not a mass market agency, look for steady exclusive relationships with large employers.

Will the company in which I'm placed treat me differently?

In some cases, yes. Certain employee benefits such as reduced lunch fee at the company cafeteria would not apply to you. In other cases, working as a consultant for a company actually helped the consultant command more respect and commitment than a full-time counterpart. Since permanent temping is becoming a way of life in many companies, the line between full-time employees (FTEs) and permanent temps is blurred.

Is it difficult to get placed?

That depends. You've become a commodity, and the speed at which you'll be placed, along with the compensation, are dependent upon the type of work you do, the demand for that type of work, and your level of proficiency and experience.

Will the agency provide healthcare benefits?

Many agencies provide healthcare benefits. However, review agency policies on eligibility. Most require a minimum amount of consecutive hours worked before becoming eligible.

What about a 401K or other retirement programs?

Some agencies provide tax deferred retirement savings, but as with healthcare benefits, there is usually an eligibility requirement.

What's the typical duration of a job?

It depends on the type of work you do and the functional level at which you're being hired. At the administrative level, many jobs are for an indefinite duration. Often, help desk technician jobs are for an indefinite period of time. At the professional level, you'll most likely be hired to fill a specific project need that can last from four to six months and the timeframe is usually defined up front. Executives are generally hired for specific projects and more lengthy durations, given the far-reaching and global nature of the executive role within an organization.

Am I eligible for paid vacation?

If you're working for an agency, vacation eligibility is dependent on a specified number of hours worked. If you're working independent of an agency, you most likely don't receive paid vacations.

How long does it take an agency to place me?

The time it takes a good agency to place you depends on the type of skills you possess, your experience level, and the demand for your skills. Early in the process, expect to hear from your agency representative every week. You should also take the initiative to stay in touch with your agency representative so that you remain visible even while you're on an assignment.

How much does it cost to list a profile on an employment site?

Most sites do not charge for you to list your resume or complete a profile. However, some sites allow one free profile and a fee for each subsequent profile. There is also a trend among certain consultant sites to restrict the best job offerings to "members only." To become a member, you would pay a monthly fee to gain access to these preferred opportunities. Carefully read the sites policies to understand if any fees apply.

Are there fees associated with obtaining a contracting position online?

Usually the listing company pays a fee to post the assignment. Some job bidding sites charge a nominal 5 percent transaction fee for assignments obtained through their site. Other job bidding sites offer optional fee-based services such as billing and collection for jobs obtained through their site.

What's the difference between 1099 and W2?

The terms 1099 and W2 describe your tax status. A 1099 is an independent contractor and responsible for paying self-employment tax (Social Security and Medicare) plus state and federal income taxes. A W2 has these taxes withheld by her employer. It's important to remember that you must meet IRS guidelines (IRS Form SS-8) for determining your status. The more control the employer exerts over directing the details of when, how, and where work is to be performed, the greater the likelihood that you fall into the W2 classification.

Can I work for an agency and still be a 1099?

When you work for an agency, you're a W2 of the agency and the agency is responsible for withholding taxes from assignments on which they place you. However, if during your association with the agency, you find other consulting assignments independent of the agency, you would then be a 1099 for those assignments and obligated to pay tax on the net income from the assignments.

What's an agency of record?

An agency of record is an agency for which you are a W2. Having an agency of record is important for consultants, especially in the technical field, who are required by the hiring company to have a third party issue paychecks and collect taxes. Many assignments in the technical field are only available to those with W2 status—meaning that you must have an agency of record.

What's an umbrella or pass-through agency?

Umbrella or pass-through agencies act as agencies of record providing the third party billing and tax withholding required by many hiring companies. Unlike temping or employment agencies, they don't find jobs for you and work on a much lower commission rate than a traditional employment agency. They basically operate like a consulting firm.

Will I be able to find temporary technical assignments without an agency of record?

It will be difficult in the technical area due to precedent-setting litigation and HR departments skittish about potential IRS audits. You can still pursue independent contractor (1099) work even though you have an agency of record. Having an agency of record will at least keep you in the running for projects from which you would have otherwise been eliminated. Explore the different agency options available before signing. You can also sign with several agencies to help increase your exposure to available projects.

What's a body shop?

A body shop is an agency that specializes in high volume, low rate, and quick turnaround assignments. They usually have a number of consultants on-call to quickly fill an immediate, but short-term need.

Where's the best place to look for temporary work?

There's no single place that provides the best opportunities. It's important to integrate several areas into your marketing plan such as Internet sites, newspapers and periodicals, industry associations, and other networking groups. Within each source, try to locate those that seem to yield the greatest or the most appropriate responses to your specific needs.

How do I determine what to charge?

This question has perplexed many novice permanent temps. You'll need to determine the method used to charge the client: hourly rate, project fee, or per diem rate.

There are several ways to determine your hourly rate, from which you can then calculate a project and per diem rate. The easiest method is to take the full-time salary for the type of work you do and divide it by 1,000 to obtain an hourly rate comparable with the benefits and perks of a full-time position. Chapter 8 provides more details on calculating rates.

Should I sign an agency agreement that includes a noncompete clause?

Agency agreements and noncompete clauses are not unusual. However, make certain you understand the extent of the limitations or restrictions before signing and seek legal advice if you're unsure. Most traditional employment agencies usually have you sign an agreement to restrict you from "stealing" their clients by negotiating an agreement directly with the client and cutting out the agency. Agencies also stipulate the terms under which you

can exit an assignment prematurely. Again, this is common practice. You need to exercise caution with the extent to which restrictions apply. An agreement should not be excessively limiting.
Remember to seek professional legal advice if you're unclear and
never succumb to pressure and hastily sign an agreement.

Should I have a signed agreement with the client?

It's always a good idea to prepare a detailed proposal for your
client. This prevents any misunderstandings and stipulates exactly
what the client is entitled to at the specified rate. Consider a can-
cellation clause also to ensure additional payment for your time
and any materials should the client cancel the project mid-stream.
This gives you a small cushion while looking for another assignment to fill the void.

Chapter 5, "Agency Agreements and Employment Contracts,"
provides additional details.

What's the best way to market myself?

First, you need to know the key benefit that you have to offer
potential clients and you should be able to articulate that in one
or two sentences (a personal deliverables statement). Answer the
client's question, "What's in it for me?"

Second, define your market and within that market space
determine what organizations will buy your services and who
within those organizations will be the main contact point.

Third, identify ways of reaching your target market and assemble a plan that integrates some or all of the available vehicles.

Look for more details in Chapter 6, "Marketing Yourself."

Can I work off-site?

Yes. Many companies offer positions for telecommuters and
home-based workers. You may be required to attend a meeting
or two. However, with the proliferation of desktop teleconferencing and high speed DSL and cable Internet connections, more

progressive companies offer video teleconferencing as an alternative to physically attending a meeting. If this is a possibility, check with your local Internet service provider to make certain that you can connect at the higher speeds required by teleconferencing technologies. If you're working through an agency, they may offer high speed Internet access to clients through their local office.

What if the company for which I'm working wants to hire me full time?

Congratulations... I think. If your goal was to work on a temporary basis as a means to find a permanent position, then congratulations are in order. However, if you're working on a temporary basis because you enjoy the temporary lifestyle, then "just say no." Whatever you decide, remember to check with your agency agreement before accepting any offers. The hiring company may have an obligation to buy out your contract or pay an agency fee to hire you as full-time regular employee.

Do I need liability insurance?

Remember, there are two types of liability insurance:

1. General liability.
2. Professional liability.

The more common general liability for error and omissions protects you from unforeseen circumstances while on company property such as a fall in the parking lot. Some companies may require general liability as a condition of employment. Professional liability protects you from personal loss in the event your services caused the employer to incur a loss. The decision to carry professional liability depends on your profession's risk factor. For example, a contract database administrator would have more liability for a failed implementation than a public relations professional. Generally, the agency agreement or contract limits the liability to a fixed amount. Chapter 8 discusses insurance.

What is the self-employment tax?

The self-employment tax (SE) refers to the Social Security and Medicare tax that is automatically withheld from the weekly paychecks of full-time employees or agency temps. In a full-time or W2 status, the employer pays a portion of the tax. However, as an independent consultant (1099 status), you are responsible for the entire 15.3 percent (12.4 percent social security plus 2.9 percent Medicare) on net earnings from $400 up to $72,600, after which certain exceptions apply.

How is the self-employment tax paid?

SE tax is paid quarterly based on your estimated net earnings (1099 earnings only) on the 15th of April, June, September, and January of the following year. You'll use form 1040 ES. See Chapter 8 for more on the tax implications of becoming a permanent temp.

What if I want to turn down a position?

You've just discovered one of the key benefits of becoming a permanent temp. Imagine trying that as a full-timer, "I'm sorry boss, but I don't think I'll accept that assignment today." If you can afford to and you're tactful and professional in doing so, then you're free to turn down any assignment. If you're turning it down because of a time constraint, first consider subcontracting or rescheduling it if the client permits. That way you will be able to retain the client and some or all of the income while working at your own pace. Of course if you're working through an agency and being paid a retainer, you may not be able to turn down an assignment so easily.

Appendix A

The following sites and references provide help information related to becoming a permanent temp.

Agencies and Internet Job Sites

Technical

www.computerwork.com.

www.dice.com.

www.industrystandard.com. (Covers all levels of technology.)

www.manpwerprofessional.com. (An agency.)

www.nettemps.com.

www.rhic.com. (RHI Consulting, an agency.)

www.Techigold.com.

Professional (agencies)

www.rhii.com. (Robert Half International includes the following divisions:

- ❖ Accountemps, Robert Half, and RHI Management Resources—specializing in accounting and finance.
- ❖ Office Team—administrative professionals.

- ❖ RHI Consulting—IT professionals.
- ❖ The Affiliates—legal professionals and paraprofessionals
- ❖ The Creative Group—creative, advertising, marketing and Web design.)

www.manpowerprofessional.com. (Manpower Professional specializes in engineering, finance, IT, scientific, telecommunications, and other professionals.)

www.brilliantpeople.com. (Management Recruiters International.)

Freelance and creative

www.ants.com.

www.aquent.com. (An agency for creative, Web, and technical.)

www.bullhorn.com.

www.freeagent.com.

www.paladinstaff.com. (An agency for marketing and advertising creatives.)

Executive

www.chiefmonster.com.

www.execunet.com.

www.executive interim management. (U.K-based organization.)

www.imcor.com. (An agency that is part of Spherion.)

www.job-bridge.com. (Interim executives.)

www.kornferry.com. (An agency.)

www.futurestep.com. (From Korn Ferry and *The Wall Street Journal*, Internet-based recruiting for middle management talent.)

www.rhimr.com. (Robert Half International—an agency. RHI Management Resources, senior level accounting and finance interim executives.)

www.startupnetworks.com. (Startup companies.)

All disciplines

www.adecco.com (agency).

www.brilliantpeople.com. (Management Recruiters International—an agency—specializing in middle-management, high-tech professionals, sales and marketing professionals, and permanent and temporary office support staff.)

www.freeagent.com.

www.hotjobs.com.

www.icplanet.com. (Specializes in independent consultants (ICs).)

www.itsyourjobnow.com.

www.joboptions.com.

www.kellyservices.com.

www.manpower.com.

www.nettemps.com.

www.norrell.com. (Now known as Spherion.)

www.sologig.com. (Fee-based listings starting at $25.00.)

www.spherion.com. (Formerly Interim Services, Inc.)

Umbrella/pass through agencies

www.Chancellor.com. (Offer sponsorship and green card obtainment assistance for Canadian TN or H-1B Visa holders.)

www.Ework.com. (Offers a variety of billing and time tracking services along with benefits.)

www.pacepros.com. (Part of Dr. James R. Ziegler's Professional Association of Contract Employees, P.A.C.E. and author of the Contract Employees Handbook at www.cehandbook.com.)

www.rmpcp.com. (RMP Consulting Partners, LLC specializing in computer and high-tech consulting.)

Career advice and planning

www.ayersgroup.com.

www.careerxroads.com. (Companion Web site to the book by Gerry Crispin and Mark Mehler.)

www.dbm.com. (Drake Beam Morin, well-known career outplacement agency.)

www.wrightassociates.com. (Outplacement agency.)

Networking Groups

www.ACG.com. (Interim positions resulting from mergers and acquisitions related.)

www.bni.com. (Business Network International.)

www.leadsclub.com. (Ali Lassen's Lead Clubs.)

www.letips.com. (LeTips.)

Message Boards

www.freelanceonline.com. (Variety of freelance professions.)

www.realrates.com/bbs. (Specializes in independent computer consultants.)

Books

General career

Crispin, Gerry and Mark Mehler. *CareerXRoads, 4th edition.* Kendall Park, NJ: MMC Group, 1999.

Kador, John. *Internet Jobs!: The Complete Guide to Finding the Hottest Internet Jobs.* New York: McGraw-Hill, 2000.

Resumes and cover letters

Kennedy, Joyce Lain. *Resumes for Dummies.* Foster City, CA: IDG Books, 1996.

Kennedy, Joyce Lain. *Cover Letters for Dummies.* Foster City, CA: IDG Books, 1996.

Contracts and legal information

Fishman, Stephen. *Consultant and Independent Contractor Agreements.* Berkeley: Nolo Press, 1998.

Fishman, Stephen. *Wage Slave No More: The Independent Contractor's Legal Guide.* Berkeley: Nolo Press, 1996.

Fishman, Stephen. *Wage Slave No More: Law and Taxes for the Self-Employed.* Berkeley: Nolo Press, 1998.

Freelance

Bly, Robert W. *Secrets of a Freelance Writer.* New York: Henry Holt and Company, 1988, 1997.

Lonier, Terry. *Working Solo: The Real Guide to Freedom and Financial Success With Your Own Business.* New Paltz, NY: Portico Press, 1994.

Ruhl, Janet. *The Computer Consultant's Guide: Real Life Strategies for Building a Successful Consulting Career.* New York: Wiley, 1994.

Time Management

Bly, Robert W. *101 Ways to Make Every Second Count: Time Management Tips and Techniques for More Success with Less Stress.* Franklin Lakes, NJ: Career Press, 1999.

Covey, Stephen R. *The Seven Habits of Highly Effective People: Restoring the Character Ethic.* New York: Simon and Schuster, 1989.

Periodicals

Business 2.0.
Business Week.
Fast Company.
Inc. Magazine.
Red Herring.

Online publications

www.1099.com. (Articles and links for independent professionals.)

www.cehandbook.com. (Contract Employees Handbook.)

www.careermag.com. (Employment and job search information.)

www.careerjournal.com. (A *Wall Street Journal* publication.)

www.careerswsj.com. (Also *The Wall Street Journal.*)

www.ceweekly.com. (Contract Employment Weekly specializing in engineering, IT/IS, and technical consulting.)

Taxes and Financial Planning

www.Irs.gov.

Visit the small business sites listed in this section. Many offer tax advice.

Salary comparisons and related sites

www.businessweek.com.

www.dbm.com/jobguide/salary.html. (This is the Riley Guide hosted on the Drake, Beam Morin site.)

www.realrates.com. (Site created by Janet Ruhl, author specializing in books on computer consulting.)

www.Salary.com.

Insurance

www.ahcpr.gov. (Agency for Healthcare Research and Quality.)

www.healthfinder.org. (U.S. Department of Health and Human Services Web site.)

www.hiaa.org. (Health Insurance Association of America.)

www.insurancenoodle.com. (Obtain information and quotes on commercial property and liability insurance.)

www.insweb.com. (Obtain information and quotes on insurance.)

www.quotesmith.com. (Obtain information and quotes on insurance.)

Search Engines

www.Altavista.com.

www.Goto.com.

www.Lycos.com.

www.Northernlights.com.

www.Yahoo.com.

Meta search sites

(Search technology that searches multiple search engines simultaneously.)

www.About.com.

www.Askjeeves.com.

www.Careerbuilder.com.

www.Dogpile.com.

www.Flipdog.com.

www.Google.com.

www.Highway61.com.

www.Jobsleuth.com.

www.Job-search-engine.com.

www.Mamma.com.

Specialty search sites

www.eresumes.com. (Rebecca Smith's eResumes & Resources.)

www.Findlaw.com. (Legal sites.)

www.Financialfind.com. (Financial sites.)

Other reference sites

www.Mediafinder.com. (Lists over 300,000 trade journals and industry periodicals.)

www.Staffing.com. (Lists staffing agencies by profession and work status.)

Keeping Yourself Marketable

Executives

www.arestydirect.wharton.upenn.edu/execed/index.cfm.

www.ExecEd@kellogg.nwu.edu.

www.exed.darden.virginia.edu/index.htm.

www.exed.hbs.edu/index.html.

www.gsb.stanford.edu/exed.

www.stern.nyu.edu/execprgms.

IS/Technology

Training and certification

www.cisco.com/warp/public/10/wwtraining.

www.ecertifications.com.

www.education.oracle.com.

www.helpdeskinst.com/hdi-certification.

www.ibm.com/services/learning.

www.microsoft.com/trainingandservices.

www.novell.com/education.

www.suned.sun.com/HQ/certification.

General software application and IT training

www.executrain.com.

www.newhorizons.com.

www.ooootraining.com (OneOnOne Computer Training).

Small Business Resources

www.Allbusiness.com (Small business services community).

www.Buyerzone.com (Small business services community).

www.Bcentral.com (Microsoft's small business portal).

www.Office.com (Small business services community).

www.Officemax.com (Office supplies and business services).

www.Onvia.com (Small business services community).

www.Sbaonline.sba.gov (U.S. Small Business Administration).

www.Score.org (Service Corps of Retired Executives provides free advice and counseling for small businesses).

www.Staples.com (Office supplies and business services).

www.Toolkit.cch.com (Small business services community).

www.Quicken.com/small_business (Small business services community from the makers of the accounting software).

Appendix B

Sample independent contractor agreement

Reproduced with permission from CCH Business Owner's Toolkit (TM) published and copyrighted by CCH INCORPORATED, 2700 Lake Cook Road, Riverwoods, IL, USA 60015, *www.toolkit.cch.com*

This Agreement is entered into as of the [_____] day of [_____], 200[ ], between _____ [company name] _____ ("the Company") and _____ [service provider's name] _____ ("the Contractor").

1.   Independent Contractor. Subject to the terms and conditions of this Agreement, the Company hereby engages the Contractor as an independent contractor to perform the services set forth herein, and the Contractor hereby accepts such engagement.

2.   Duties, Term, and Compensation. The Contractor's duties, term of engagement, compensation and provisions for payment thereof shall be as set forth in the estimate previously provided to the Company by the Contractor and which is attached as Exhibit A, which may be amended in writing from time to time, or supplemented with subsequent estimates for services to be rendered by the Contractor and agreed to by the Company, and which collectively are hereby incorporated by reference.

3.   Expenses. During the term of this Agreement, the Contractor shall bill and the Company shall reimburse [him or her] for all

reasonable and approved out-of-pocket expenses which are incurred in connection with the performance of the duties hereunder. Notwithstanding the foregoing, expenses for the time spend by Consultant in traveling to and from Company facilities shall not be reimbursable.

4.   Written Reports. The Company may request that project plans, progress reports and a final results report be provided by Consultant on a monthly basis. A final results report shall be due at the conclusion of the project and shall be submitted to the Company in a confidential written report at such time. The results report shall be in such form and setting forth such information and data as is reasonably requested by the Company.

5.   Inventions. Any and all inventions, discoveries, developments and innovations conceived by the Contractor during this engagement relative to the duties under this Agreement shall be the exclusive property of the Company; and the Contractor hereby assigns all right, title, and interest in the same to the Company. Any and all inventions, discoveries, developments and innovations conceived by the Contractor prior to the term of this Agreement and utilized by [him or her] in rendering duties to the Company are hereby licensed to the Company for use in its operations and for an infinite duration. This license is non-exclusive, and may be assigned without the Contractor's prior written approval by the Company to a wholly-owned subsidiary of the Company.

6.   Confidentiality. The Contractor acknowledges that during the engagement [he or she] will have access to and become acquainted with various trade secrets, inventions, innovations, processes, information, records and specifications owned or licensed by the Company and/or used by the Company in connection with the operation of its business including, without limitation, the Company's business and product processes, methods, customer lists, accounts and procedures. The Contractor agrees that [he or she] will not disclose any of the aforesaid, directly or indirectly, or use any of them in any manner, either during the term of this Agreement or at any time thereafter, except as required in the course of this engagement with the Company. All files, records, documents, blueprints, specifications, information, letters, notes, media lists, original artwork/creative, notebooks, and similar items relating to the business of the Company,

whether prepared by the Contractor or otherwise coming into [his or her] possession, shall remain the exclusive property of the Company. The Contractor shall not retain any copies of the foregoing without the Company's prior written permission. Upon the expiration or earlier termination of this Agreement, or whenever requested by the Company, the Contractor shall immediately deliver to the Company all such files, records, documents, specifications, information, and other items in [his or her] possession or under [his or her] control. The Contractor further agrees that [he or she] will not disclose [his or her] retention as an independent contractor or the terms of this Agreement to any person without the prior written consent of the Company and shall at all times preserve the confidential nature of [his or her] relationship to the Company and of the services hereunder.

7.   Conflicts of Interest; Non-hire Provision. The Contractor represents that [he or she] is free to enter into this Agreement, and that this engagement does not violate the terms of any agreement between the Contractor and any third party. Further, the Contractor, in rendering [his or her] duties shall not utilize any invention, discovery, development, improvement, innovation, or trade secret in which [he or she] does not have a proprietary interest. During the term of this agreement, the Contractor shall devote as much of [his or her] productive time, energy and abilities to the performance of [his or her] duties hereunder as is necessary to perform the required duties in a timely and productive manner. The Contractor is expressly free to perform services for other parties while performing services for the Company. For a period of six months following any termination, the Contractor shall not, directly or indirectly hire, solicit, or encourage to leave the Company's employment, any employee, consultant, or contractor of the Company or hire any such employee, consultant, or contractor who has left the Company's employment or contractual engagement within one year of such employment or engagement.

8.   Right to Injunction. The parties hereto acknowledge that the services to be rendered by the Contractor under this Agreement and the rights and privileges granted to the Company under the Agreement are of a special, unique, unusual, and extraordinary character which gives them a peculiar value, the loss of which cannot be reasonably or adequately compensated by damages in any action at law, and the breach by the Contractor of any of the provisions of this

Agreement will cause the Company irreparable injury and damage. The Contractor expressly agrees that the Company shall be entitled to injunctive and other equitable relief in the event of, or to prevent, a breach of any provision of this Agreement by the Contractor. Resort to such equitable relief, however, shall not be construed to be a waiver of any other rights or remedies that the Company may have for damages or otherwise. The various rights and remedies of the Company under this Agreement or otherwise shall be construed to be cumulative, and no one of the them shall be exclusive of any other or of any right or remedy allowed by law.

9. Merger. This Agreement shall not be terminated by the merger of consolidation of the Company into or with any other entity.

10. Termination. The Company may terminate this Agreement at any time by 10 working days' written notice to the Contractor. In addition, if the Contractor is convicted of any crime or offense, fails or refuses to comply with the written policies or reasonable directive of the Company, is guilty of serious misconduct in connection with performance hereunder, or materially breaches provisions of this Agreement, the Company at any time may terminate the engagement of the Contractor immediately and without prior written notice to the Contractor.

11. Independent Contractor. This Agreement shall not render the Contractor an employee, partner, agent of, or joint venturer with the Company for any purpose. The Contractor is and will remain an independent contractor in [his or her] relationship to the Company. The Company shall not be responsible for withholding taxes with respect to the Contractor's compensation hereunder. The Contractor shall have no claim against the Company hereunder or otherwise for vacation pay, sick leave, retirement benefits, social security, worker's compensation, health or disability benefits, unemployment insurance benefits, or employee benefits of any kind.

12. Insurance. The Contractor will carry liability insurance (including malpractice insurance, if warranted) relative to any service that [he or she] performs for the Company.

13. Successors and Assigns. All of the provisions of this Agreement shall be binding upon and inure to the benefit of the parties hereto and their respective heirs, if any, successors, and assigns.

14. Choice of Law. The laws of the state of [_____] shall govern the validity of this Agreement, the construction of its terms and the interpretation of the rights and duties of the parties hereto.

15. Arbitration. Any controversies arising out of the terms of this Agreement or its interpretation shall be settled in [_____] in accordance with the rules of the American Arbitration Association, and the judgment upon award may be entered in any court having jurisdiction thereof.

16. Headings. Section headings are not to be considered a part of this Agreement and are not intended to be a full and accurate description of the contents hereof.

17. Waiver. Waiver by one party hereto of breach of any provision of this Agreement by the other shall not operate or be construed as a continuing waiver.

18. Assignment. The Contractor shall not assign any of [his or her] rights under this Agreement, or delegate the performance of any of [his or her] duties hereunder, without the prior written consent of the Company.

19. Notices. Any and all notices, demands, or other communications required or desired to be given hereunder by any party shall be in writing and shall be validly given or made to another party if personally served, or if deposited in the United States mail, certified or registered, postage prepaid, return receipt requested. If such notice or demand is served personally, notice shall be deemed constructively made at the time of such personal service. If such notice, demand or other communication is given by mail, such notice shall be conclusively deemed given five days after deposit thereof in the United States mail addressed to the party to whom such notice, demand or other communication is to be given as follows:

If to the Contractor:	[name]
	[street address]
	[city, state, zip]
If to the Company:	[name]
	[street address]
	[city, state, zip]

Any party hereto may change its address for purposes of this paragraph by written notice given in the manner provided above.

20. Modification or Amendment. No amendment, change or modification of this Agreement shall be valid unless in writing signed by the parties hereto.

21. Entire Understanding. This document and any exhibit attached constitute the entire understanding and agreement of the parties, and any and all prior agreements, understandings, and representations are hereby terminated and canceled in their entirety and are of no further force and effect.

22. Unenforceability of Provisions. If any provision of this Agreement, or any portion thereof, is held to be invalid and unenforceable, then the remainder of this Agreement shall nevertheless remain in full force and effect.

IN WITNESS WHEREOF the undersigned have executed this Agreement as of the day and year first written above. The parties hereto agree that facsimile signatures shall be as effective as if originals.

[company name]	[contractor's name]
By: _____	By: _____
Its: [title or position]	Its: [title or position]

SCHEDULE A

DUTIES, TERM, AND COMPENSATION

DUTIES

The Contractor will _____ [describe here the work or service to be performed]_____ .

[He or she] will report directly to _____ [name]_____ and to any other party designated by _____ [name]_____ in connection with the performance of the duties under this Agreement and shall fulfill any other duties reasonably requested by the Company and agreed to by the Contractor.

TERM

This engagement shall commence upon execution of this Agreement and shall continue in full force and effect through ____ [date]_____ or earlier upon completion of the Contractor's duties under this Agreement. The Agreement may only be extended thereafter by mutual agreement, unless terminated earlier by operation of and in accordance with this Agreement.

COMPENSATION (Choose A or B)

A. As full compensation for the services rendered pursuant to this Agreement, the Company shall pay the Contractor at the hourly rate of __[dollar amount]__ per hour, with total payment not to exceed __[dollar amount]__ without prior written approval by an authorized representative of the Company. Such compensation shall be payable within 30 days of receipt of Contractor's monthly invoice for services rendered supported by reasonable documentation.

B. As full compensation for the services rendered pursuant to this Agreement, the Company shall pay the Contractor the sum of _[dollar amount]_ , to be paid _____ [time and conditions of payment]_____ .

Bibliography

Bly, Robert W. *101 Ways to Make Every Second Count: Time Management Tips and Techniques for More Success with Less Stress.* Franklin Lakes, NJ: Career Press, 1999.

———. *Secrets of a Freelance Writer.* New York: Henry Holt and Company, 1988, 1997.

Cohen, Sacha, and Neil Carlson, "Dr. Robert Reich Discusses the Future of eWorking," *www.ework.com*, October, 2000.

Covey, Stephen R. *The Seven Habits of Highly Effective People: Restoring the Character Ethic.* New York: Simon and Schuster, 1989.

Crispin, Gerry and Mark Mehler. *CareerXRoads, 4th edition.* Kendall Park, NJ: MMC Group, 1999.

Editors of Career Press. *101 Great Resumes.* Franklin Lakes, NJ: Career Press, 1996.

Fein, Richard. *Cover Letters! Cover Letters! Cover Letters!.* Franklin Lakes, NJ: Career Press, 1996

Fishman, Stephen. *Consultant and Independent Contractor Agreements.* Berkeley: Nolo Press, 1998.

———. *Wage Slave No More: Law and Taxes for the Self-Employed.* Berkeley: Nolo Press, 1998.

———. *Wage Slave No More: The Independent Contractor's Legal Guide.* Berkeley: Nolo Press, 1996.

Fry, Ron. *101 Great Answers to the Toughest Interview Questions.* Franklin Lakes, NJ: Career Press, 1991.

Greenhouse, Steven. "Microsoft Settles Suit With Temp Workers," *The New York Times on the Web*, December 13, 2000.

Internal Revenue Service, *Publication 15A, Employers Supplemental Tax Guide; Who Are Employees?*

Justice, Peggy O'Connell. *The Temp Track.* Princeton: Peterson's, 1994.

Kador, John. *Internet Jobs!: The Complete Guide to Finding the Hottest Internet Jobs.* New York: McGraw-Hill, 2000.

Kennedy, Joyce Lain. *Cover Letters for Dummies.* Foster City, CA: IDG Books, 1996.

———. *Resumes for Dummies.* Foster City, CA: IDG Books, 1996.

Lieber, Ron. "The Permatemps Contretemps," *Fast Company*, August 2000: 200, 203, 214.

Lonier, Terry. *Working Solo: The Real Guide to Freedom and Financial Success With Your Own Business.* New Paltz, NY: Portico Press, 1994.

Ruhl, Janet. *The Computer Consultant's Guide: Real Life Strategies for Building a Successful Consulting Career.* New York: Wiley, 1994.

Silvestri, George T. "Employment Outlook 1996-2006,"*Monthly Labor Review.* November, 1997, 58-59, 77.

Smith, Rebecca. *Rebecca Smith's eResumes & Resources, www.eresumes.com*.

U.S. Department of Labor Bureau of Labor Statistics, "Are Workers More Secure?" *Issues in Labor Statistics*, May, 1998.

———. "Contingent and Alternative Work Arrangements," February, 1999.

Wendleton, Kate. *Building a Great Resume.* Franklin Lakes, NJ: Career Press, 1999.

Ziegler, Dr. James R. *The Contract Employees Handbook. www.cehandbook.com*, 2000. pacepros.com – part of Dr. James R.

Index

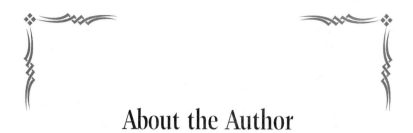

About the Author

Joan Damico is a freelance business writer and consultant specializing in business-to-business high tech and industrial marketing. Her work has appeared in several domestic and international trade journals and business publications such as *The Business 2 Business Marketer, Automotive Technologies International, Plastics Solutions*, and *Inpra Latina* covering a variety of technology and business related topics.

Joan holds a business degree in organizational resource management with a concentration in communications. As an independent professional, Joan has worked with clients who have successfully implemented contingent staffing programs. She has a first hand look at the issues and opportunities facing independent consultants. Joan is the founder and president of J. Damico Marketing Communications and resides in Walden, NY. She can be reached at joan@jdamico.net.